BRIDGE FOR IMPROVERS

DERREK STUBBINGS &
HOWARD MELBOURNE

The Crowood Press

First published in 1989 by
The Crowood Press
Ramsbury, Marlborough,
Wiltshire SN8 2HR

This impression 1992

British Library Cataloguing in Publication Data

Stubbings, Derrek
Bridge for improvers.
1. Contract bridge. Manuals
I. Title II. Melbourne, Howard
795.41'5

ISBN 1 85223 184 X

Typeset by Consort Art Graphics, Exeter, Devon
Printed in Great Britain by Biddles Ltd, of Guildford and Kings' Lynn

Contents

Foreword

In my opinion, bridge is the most fascinating game of cards ever invented. You cannot fail to be captivated and enthralled by the magic of this game of skill, logic and luck. Apart from being a very sociable game, it continually stimulates the mind, and even the experts are always learning something new. This book will teach you all the basic rules for playing a good game of bridge, but remember – no one bridge book can teach you everything. Many a good player will have started by reading a book such as this, which explains all you need to know to be able to enjoy a game, but of course you can never learn everything just by reading. You have to play whilst learning to be able to fully appreciate every aspect of the game – and this book will certainly help you to do just that.

Michelle Brunner
World Ladies' Champion 1985

Preface

Our main aim has been to make this a readable book, one that you find it easy to come back to and not difficult to understand. We have gone for basic principles which will stand you in good stead throughout your bridge career, whilst keeping the work sufficiently technical to quieten the purists and, more importantly, to introduce you to technicality gently enough for it to be bearable.

We should mention Chapters 3, 4 and 5. We divided a pack of cards into two, and from one half dealt the hands in Chapter 3 on opening bids, and from the other dealt the hands in Chapter 4 on responses. This has enabled us to set the hands in one chapter off against various hands from the other to show you the great variety of situations which can arise at the table. This is done in Chapter 5, the complete uncontested bidding sequence.

As a result, many situations are met in the book which you may not be able to deal with so well at the present stage of your bridge experience. But these *are* situations which you may well meet at the table. The pack doesn't know you can't cope with awkward hands yet, and will throw up the usual quota of them. So we have explained thoroughly all the things you should be taking seriously right now, and included glimpses into the future. We think this better than leaving you to suppose that all hands are simple, and then having you flounder hopelessly at the table because you cannot find anything at all in the book to give you a clue how to cope. Too many 'elementary' bridge books leave the reader in this position and we are sure you will prefer our honesty. If when you are reading you find some of the hands more than you want to cope with yet, leave them until later. Use your own judgement! However, when at the table some wretchedly impossible hand crops up, then you may well be able to find a clue within these pages. To help you in this process we have included a glossary of all the hands in the book (*see* page 172), so when a hand poses a problem, simply read through the list until you find one somewhat like it, note where in the book it appears, and look it up.

Because of space problems, we were unable to add 'prep' questions throughout Chapter 5. Before reading what we have to say about responding with a particular hand, therefore, and the subsequent bidding, ask yourself some questions. What would you respond on 'this' hand if partner opened 1C 1D 1H 1S 1NT. You will then be able to compare your answers with our advice.

Based on the teaching experience of the authors, the book should lend itself well to use by classes in further education.

There is one unusual notation we use, and it is only fair to warn you. The usual notation for a ten is 10 since this is how it appears on the actual card. For two reasons, either sufficient in itself we believe, we write:

ten = T

First, a ten is an honour card, like A K Q J, and the single letter usage reminds us of this; second, the ten is the only card not usually represented by a single symbol:

A K Q J 10 9 8 7 6 5 4 3 2

A written array representing a hand looks much more tidy and is therefore much more easy to scan if the vertical columns are all regular, as they are with our notation. Unfortunately, in the printing of this book we could not meet this requirement, but we suggest you try it in your own longhand when you write, and you'll see what we mean.

1 What Sort of a Game is Bridge?

Well, it's not like chess or ludo, for a start. It's different from the former and more complex than the latter. There are an enormous number of possible deals available from a pack of fifty-two cards. So many, indeed, that you are unlikely to meet the same deal twice in your lifetime. Furthermore, at the end of the deal the cards are face down on the table, and even after you have picked up your hand and looked at it you have only seen one-quarter of the deal. The other three-quarters are largely unknown; not entirely, because you know they do not contain any of the cards in your hand.

Compare this with chess, where you know the whole starting position every time, and it is always the same. Also, you expect one game of chess to take an hour or two. In bridge you face a new start position every five or ten minutes, and in that time you have, to the best of your present ability, to:

(a) **assess** your hand;
(b) look for ways to **inform** your partner;
(c) **listen** to what your partner *and the opposition* have to say, and then adjust your assessment accordingly;
(d) make, or read, the **opening lead**;
(e) **follow** the subsequent play, placing more and more of the remaining cards in the other hands, or not, as the case may be;
(f) make several **decisions** in the bidding, and in the play.

What bridge has in common with ludo is the element of chance which in chess is eliminated by the fixed start noted above. For many people this adds an extra element of excitement or fascination. Bridge is a dynamic game, not a static one, demanding as much concentration to play well as chess, although in different ways. There is plenty of room for mistakes to be made, but by the same token there is endless room for improvement and the satisfaction to be gained therefrom.

There are **patterns** in bridge, just as there are patterns in chess. There are patterns in bidding, patterns in card holdings, and patterns in play.

In reading about bridge you have become accustomed to seeing a written representation of a hand. Occasionally you have seen the whole deal displayed. We suspect that you have found conclusions easier to reach, or to understand, when the complete deal has been available. Analysis of a deal with all the cards shown is called double dummy. This is a term worth learning. Such an analysis can be done at the bridge table. It can aid learning to undertake a postmortem on a double dummy basis by turning all the cards face up at the end of play. To this end it is worth practising the method used in competitive play; to do this from the start gives you the added advantage that when you meet it later you will not be a stranger to it. Instead of throwing all four cards of a trick together, learn to place your own cards in front of you, turning each card face down as the trick is completed. If the card was in a winning trick place it upright, so:

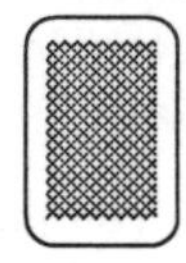

and if in a losing trick place it sideways, so:

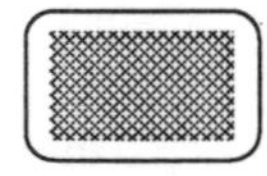

It is then easy at the end of a game to see which pairs won which tricks. For instance, the arrays below show that the EW partnership won tricks 2, 3, 4, 7, 8, 11 and lost the others. NS won tricks 1, 5, 6, 9, 10, 12, 13. In front of east (and west) lies the array:

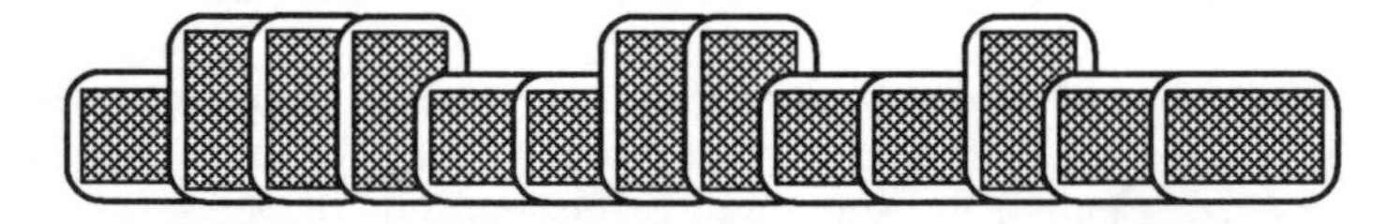

while in front of north (and south) there will be the array:

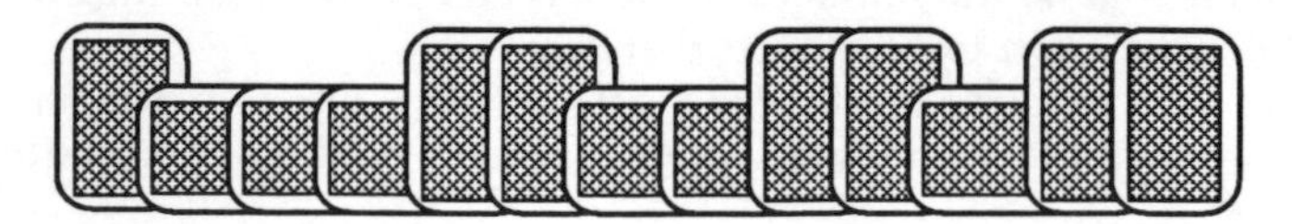

There is an element of probability (that is, assessment of chance) involved in most of the calculations you have to make. In few situations do you *know*

exactly how many points a particular player has,
exactly how many cards in a particular suit,
whether or not that suit contains a particular card,

and so on. However, you should, as the weeks and the hands go by, begin to **assess the chances**, and do so with increasing success. Where in chess you ask:

'If opponent moves *that,* what then . . .?'

in bridge it is usual to have to start with the question:

'If opponent *holds* that, what then . . .?'

There is, therefore, some **counting** to be done if you are to be entirely aware of what is going on in any hand. Some people are discouraged by this, but we believe that no one element of the counting scene is unduly difficult. What will not be so easy until you've had some practice is keeping several counts going at once. We think it worthwhile, therefore, to show you more carefully than most writers how to set about counting. We shall show you most aspects of counting in this book, but we suggest you set about mastering them one at a time. The first, probably, is remembering how many cards have gone and how many are to come, but there are others. It is likely that the more you understand how to use the count the easier it will be to count so we must try to show you. For instance:

(a)	Opponent bids	**1H: count**	13–21	points
			4+	hearts (4 or more)
(b)	and rebids	2H: **recount**	12–15	points
			5+	hearts

Or a different sort of example, in which we assume normal leads:

(c) Partner leads ♠4 to a NT contract and you hold the ♠3
count 4/5 spades

This is not all, it is only a beginning. *Now look at your hand.* You see:

K 7 3	and **count**	6 points
Q T 4 2		3 spades
8 6		4 hearts
J 8 7 3		

Make a table in your mind, like this:

		You	Bidder	You+Bidder
(a)	points	6	13–21	19–27
	hearts	4	4+	8+

You still haven't finished. You have only reached part totals. There are forty points and thirteen hearts in the deal. Thus:

	Total	You+Bidder	Two other players share
points	40	19–27	21–13
hearts	13	8+	5– (five or less)

Your partner has some share of possibly half the points in the deal, and there must be a doubleton heart out, if not a singleton or void. You will confirm this as hearts are played.

We leave you to do the detailed counting in cases (b) and (c), but after you have been through a similar series of steps you should conclude that two other players share:

(b) 22–19 points 4– hearts

(c) 6/5 spades

Many players begin the count, but then fail to complete it, thus failing to make adequate use of it.

There are deductions to be made at every step and, as your experience grows and you find it correspondingly easier to remember, you will be able to make more and more of them. No one who is sensible will expect you to make them straight away, but as you manage each step *at the table* for the first time a kind of warm glow occurs somewhere inside.

East opens 1NT (13–15 balanced); your partner sitting South overcalls 2D, and you, holding

K T 8 2
(N) A J 2
8 4
Q J 8 3

bid 2NT. Partner raises to three. East leads the ♥K and dummy goes down with:

(S)		count		
	A J 3		you	11
	8 5 3		partner	15
	A Q J 7 2		partnership total	26
	K 4		total	40
			opponents	14

But opener's bid shows 13–15, so in fact opener has either 13 or 14, with West holding either 1 or 0. Now J=1, and you can see every J in the deal, so West holds 0 and every high card missing is held by East, who will have no singleton. You can therefore **construct the whole deal** in your mind (see below) and play it double dummy in effect.

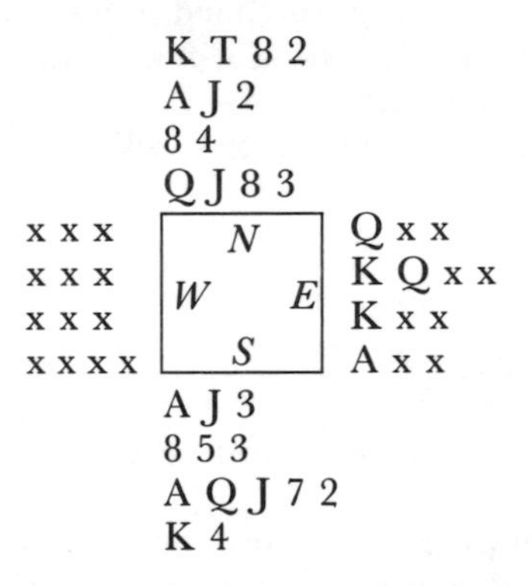

Your first decision has to be whether to take the ♥K or to duck it. Experiment, and decide which is best. We shall return to this hand in the chapter on play (Chapter 11).

After the bidding sequence:

S	W	N	E
1H	4C	4H	4S
5H	–	–	–

and the lead of the ♣K you, sitting South, see:

7 6 3
K 9 8 6 2
5
A 7 3 2

♣K

A 5 2
A Q J T 7 3
A 9 6
9

There are only two hearts missing, so even if they break 2–0 two rounds will draw them, leaving three trumps in dummy to cover ♦9 and ♦6, and four trumps in hand to cover the ♣7, ♣3 and ♣2. It looks as if the hand is cold for eleven tricks, losing two spades. How do you play it? We shall come back to this hand in the chapter on play.

Even when you cannot make a bid, and partner does not either, still count. If the opposition have stopped in 2D there is an inference. They probably hold no more than 23 points between them, possibly less.

$$40 - 23 = 17$$

You hold 7 points only, and are inclined to lose interest, but *complete* the count. $17 - 7 = 10$. Partner at worst still has quite a reasonable hand, so wake up and give some support.

The basic principle, as in poker or blackjack, is to ask of any bid or play:

'What can I gain . . .
what can I lose . . .
what are the odds . . .?'

and then **back the odds** year in and year out to become a consistent winner.

To achieve this happy position you must gradually learn to count and to make sensible deductions from your conclusions. In this book we shall try to show you how.

So bridge has the following characteristics:

- it is a **dynamic** game;
- it is a **partnership** game;
- it is based on **probability**;
- each hand falls into stages – **bidding** – opening, middle, and end game **play**;
- it has room for **psychology** and all the other attributes of any good game;
- above all, it requires **judgement**.

2 Assessment of the Hand

You have already learned to count A=4, K=3, Q=2, J=1, and a little about counting length. Now we need to realise just how rough a measure that is, even while we go on using it. A king looks a very good card, but when the opposition have the ace your king will only make part of the time, depending upon such things as which side the ace lies. Again, in a trump contract your king may be ruffed, while when the opposition reel off two long suits in NT you may be forced into the ignominy of discarding the wretched thing, and on a 2 at that! By the same token, nines and tens, which you haven't learned to count, quite frequently earn tricks.

We do have to use some yardstick, however, and the 4, 3, 2, 1 count is almost universal as a starter. It is a basis upon which to build, a point from which to begin (unfortunately, for some it is also an end). There are strong hands and weak, balanced hands and unbalanced, hands which fit with partner and hands which are a chronic misfit.

We have to start somewhere, so consider the following deal. It is an unlikely deal in practice, for it requires the pack to be stacked in order from the two of clubs to the ace of spades. Try it yourself, and you will obtain the rotationally symmetrical deal shown. Every hand has ten points, every hand has one of each denomination of card, each partnership has exactly the same suit combinations. Yet tricks are indivisible, so one partnership or the other, in play in NT, would have to come to more than six tricks. It becomes obvious that there must be factors other than points, or distribution, which affect the outcome of any hand.

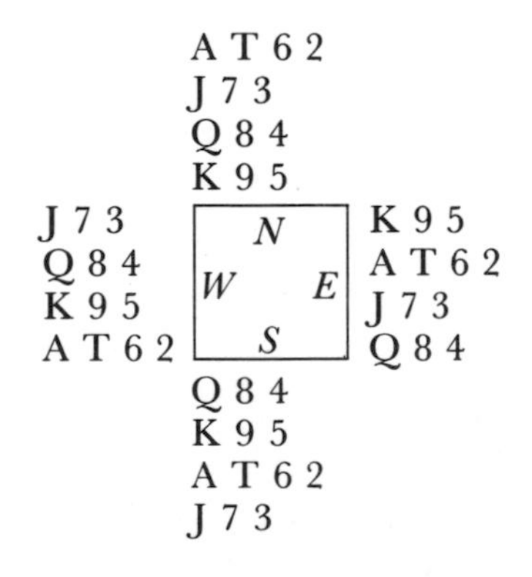

There is the matter of who is on lead, and what they lead. There is an item of considerable importance called **timing**. That is, *when* you choose to play a certain card. Look again at the hands on pages 10–12. *When* are you going to play the ♥A in the one case and the ♣A in the other? Then there is the matter of partnership. A pair who play for each other will always score over a pair who refuse to listen to one another.

There is something called *bias* which needs to be understood. In the hand above every suit has either three or four cards in it. The number of cards in a suit is called its **length**. Lengths of three and four cards are called normal. When there are fewer the suit is called **short**, and when there are more it is called **long**. Obviously, shortages vary through 2/1/0, while length varies from 5 to a most improbable 13. A hand with a combination of shortage and length is usually best played with a long suit as trumps, while a moderately balanced hand is usually better played in NT. Consider hands 1–8, where the notation for bias, counting upwards from four or downwards from three, is our own: S++ = 4 + 2 = 6 card spade suit; H– = 3 – 1 = 2 card heart suit.

	K J 8 3	K Q J 8 3	A	T 8 4
	Q 7 4	Q 7 4	Q T 9 7 4 3	K
	T 6 5	6 5	K T 6 5	A Q 8 7 5
	J 8 4	Q J 4	K 4	J 8 6 4
	7	11	12	(7)
		S+ D–	S–– H++ C–	H–– D+
	4 3 3 3	5 3 2 3	1 6 4 2	3 1 5 4
Hand:	**1**	**2**	**3**	**4**

J T 7 5 3	A J 7 6 4	A Q 7	7
A K	T 9	K Q J 6	A K Q T 8 7 6 3
Q T 8 6	A K 7 4	K Q 8	–
A Q	A 3	A K Q	K Q J 6
16	16	26	15
S+ H– C–	S+ H– C–		S–– H++++ D–––
5 2 4 2	5 2 4 2	3 4 3 3	1 8 0 4
5	**6**	**7**	**8**

Hands 1 and 7 are unbiased, while all the others are biased. A hand is **balanced** if it has no more than one +/–, like hands 1, 2, 7. It is **semi balanced** if it contains two doubletons, like hands 5 and 6. Others are **unbalanced.** In a very real sense the + biases are the consequences of the – ones, and vice versa. They are two sides of the same coin – there is only *one* coin.

Note the initial score allotted to hand 4. Until partner has bid hearts, either directly or concealed within a NT bid, it is better to discount the K value of the singleton until you have more experience. Once the ♥A is led it has no more value than any other singleton. Once partner has made a bid which warrants it, however, three points may be added back into the high card score. Note, though, that in NT there is a disadvantage to be aware of in the shortage if partner hasn't bid hearts directly – opponents may have long hearts to cash if they can establish them and get in. If this is the case you must have tricks which you can make *in time.* The singleton K in hand 4 is an obvious case, but you should always be alert to the way the bidding affects your hand and hence your assessment of it. For instance, if you hold ♦K8 and diamonds are bid *strongly* on your right then your K becomes a more likely trick, whilst if there is similar bidding on your left it becomes a less likely trick, and your hand becomes worth three points less.

J T 7 5 3	A J 7 6 4	A Q 7	7
A K	T 9	K Q J 6	A K Q T 8 7 6 3
Q T 8 6	A K 7 4	K Q 8	–
A Q	A 3	A K Q	K Q J 6
5	**6**	**7**	**8**

The analysis beneath the hands on page 14 makes hands 5 and 6 seem identical in value; however, you should be aware of a major difference between them. In hand 5 thirteen of the points are in the two doubletons, which will make suit establishment more difficult for you and less difficult for opponents.

As a last point, look back at hands 7 and 8. Hand 8, played in hearts, is surely worth ten tricks even with no support from partner's hand at all, yet with eleven points more, hand 7, without help from partner, will find it very difficult to make more than seven tricks. Such is the potential playing power of distribution. Defence, however, puts a different slant on things. It should be easy enough to see that hand 8 will have little or no defensive value against a hand stacked with spades and diamonds playing in a spade contract.

Now look again at the artificial deal shown on page 13. Get a pack of cards and reproduce it in front of you. Give North the three jacks from E, S, W and replace them with small or intermediate cards from North's hand. The points distribution is now:

N	S	E	W	N+S	E+W
13	9	9	9	22	18

and the difference between the NS total and that for EW is 4, worth one ace. If the deal is still to be played in NT there is every chance that it will be NS who take the extra trick. Obviously partner may not hold nine points, but the occasions when partner holds less will be balanced by those when partner holds more. Remember, we are assessing *chance*, and the odds are in your favour now. You cannot leave partner ignorant of the joyful news, so you must find an opening bid.

If you proceed, step by step, to move one point from each of the other hands into North's hand, just as we have already done, swapping, say, a K for a Q now the Js have gone, you will obtain the results shown below. Remember, this is only a rough calculation, and it is constructed from and for balanced hands. It does not take into account which side of kings the aces lie, it being usual to suppose that the various factors will balance out. When they don't they either tip in your favour ('good luck') or away from you ('bad luck'). The last line of the table is separated from the body to indicate that it breaks down at that level. The eight points missing can represent two aces, which preclude a successful slam except on the occasions where you play in a suit and you or partner are void opposite one of them. We shall return to this problem in Chapter 9.

Once you have learned the **totals v trick expectation** in this table it only remains for us to point out two things. First, a total of 26 can just as easily be made up of, say 13+13, or 11+15. The second is that allowance should be made for distribution. We shall discuss this again later.

N	E	S	W	N+S	E+W	**Diff**	**Likely trick expectation**	**Open**
10	10	10	10	20	20	0	7/6	–
13	9	9	9	22	18	4=1A	7	1
16	8	8	8	24	16	8=2A	8	1
19	7	7	7	26	14	12=3A	9	1
22	6	6	6	28	12	16=4A	10	2
25	5	5	5	30	10	20=5A	11	2
28	4	4	4	32	8 !!			

Now we must assess distributional values. If you are going to play in *your* suit, or in NT expecting to make your long cards after opponents' holding is exhausted, one method is to add a point for each card after the fourth. Thus, looking at the hands on page 14,

K Q J 8 3	A
Q 7 4	Q T 9 7 4 3
6 5	K T 6 5
Q J 4	K 4
2	**3**

hand 2, playing in spades, can now be counted as 12;
hand 3, playing in hearts, can now be counted as 14.

Note that this method is in effect adding one for each + attached to your suit in the analysis. Another method utilises the –s elsewhere in the analysis on page 14. Adding a point for each of these to the original score has the following effect:
hand 2, playing in spades, can be counted as 12, as before;
hand 3, playing in hearts, can now be counted as 15, not 14.

In effect you are adding one point for each doubleton, two for each singleton, and three for each void. Note that each method evaluates hand 2 the same, but that the latter method favours hand 3 slightly. To get a better impression of the difference between the two methods consider hands 5 and 8 playing in spades and hearts respectively:

Hand	1st method	2nd method
5	17	18
8	19	20

J T 7 5 3	7
A K	A K Q T 8 7 6 3
Q T 8 6	–
A Q	K Q J 6
5	**8**

Remember that what we are trying to assess is the strength added to the hand by the power to ruff. Now a five card suit, without undue support from partner, will not have many ruffs available after drawing trumps, especially if the outstanding trumps are adversely distributed. The occasional wretched hand where you set out blithely to draw trumps, holding five in your own hand and two in dummy, only to have opponent on your right show out on the first round, revealing opponent on your left to have more trumps than you! So with simply a five card suit be cautious, and do not add your one until partner supports, after which you can afford to use the shortage method. We deal with this aspect of assessment more thoroughly in Chapter 3.

A Q 7	7
K Q J 6	A K Q T 8 7 6 3
K Q 8	–
A K Q	K Q J 6
7	**8**

On the other hand, comparing the **playing strengths** of hands 7 and 8 again, it isn't difficult to see that neither method alone gives an adequate impression of the playing strength of hand 8 in a heart contract. Here, both methods combined offer a revised count of 24, which is a much truer comparison with the ostensible strength of hand 7.

So how do you tell? Most writers will give you simple rules of thumb, when what is needed is judgement. Looking at hand 8 again, note that only five trumps are missing, to be divided among three other players. You will be unfortunate indeed not to be able to draw trumps *and* have five, or even six, trumps left with which to control the hand. In order to learn judgement in these situations make a record of when you are disastrously wrong in your assessment, whichever way your error lies, jotting down the hands. You should be able to spot the combinations you are regularly over or under valuing, and then deduce why.

There are other methods with hands such as hand 8, which is probably why other writers ignore the discussion above (or maybe it is to avoid this discussion that other methods have been invented). We shall introduce you to them in Chapter 7.

Before going on to Chapters 3 and 4, opening the bidding and responding to partner's opening bid, try a run through the following hands. For now, try to answer these four questions on each hand:

1 How many points are there in the hand?
2 Is there any bias in the hand? If so, what is it?
3 Would you open the bidding on the hand? If so, how?
4 Partner opens 1H and next player passes; what do you say?

A		**B**		**C**		**D**	
	K 5		T 8		Q 9 3		9 4 3
	T 3		J 9 7		Q 5		A K T 8 3
	A Q T 9 8 3		J T 9 7		K 7 5 2		6 2
	6 5 4		K 7 3 2		J 8 3 2		T 8 6
1	......		......		......		......
2	......		......		......		......
3	......		......		......		......
4	......		......		......		......

E		**F**		**G**		**H**	
	A T 7 4 2		2		J 8 6		K Q 7 6 3
	9		Q 7		A K J 8 7 6 4 2		A K 2
	J 6 4		A K 5 2		–		J 9
	Q T 9 7		A Q T 9 8 5		A K		K J 6
1	......		......		......		......
2	......		......		......		......
3	......		......		......		......
4	......		......		......		......

J		**K**		**L**		**M**	
	K Q 5 3		A J T 8 5 4		9 7 6		9
	Q 8 7		9 8 4 3		J 4 3 2		J T 6 5
	8		8 7		J 6 5 2		Q T 6 4 3
	K J 7 6 5		7		9 3		4 3 2
1	......		......		......		......
2	......		......		......		......
3	......		......		......		......
4	......		......		......		......

N		**P**		**Q**		**R**	
	A T 4 2		A T 9 5		J 8		K 8 7
	9 5		7 6 4		A K T 6		9 8
	K Q T 9 3		K T 8		A 7 4		A Q 9 2
	8 4		A J 3		A Q T 2		K Q 8 7
1	......		......		......		......
2	......		......		......		......
3	......		......		......		......
4	......		......		......		......

S		**T**		**U**		**V**	
	K Q 5		Q 6 4 3		A J 7 6 2		J 2
	6 4 2		K Q T 5 2		Q 5		A J 3
	A 4 3		7 6		K Q 8 5		J 5 4 3
	A Q J 5		T 2		9 4		9 6 5 4
1	......		......		......		......
2	......		......		......		......
3	......		......		......		......
4	......		......		......		......

3 Opening the Bidding at the One Level

HANDS WITH BALANCED DISTRIBUTION

If you possess a hand with balanced distribution you shouldn't open the bidding unless you can see a rebid over any unlimited response from partner. When you open with one of a suit you show partner that you hold at least four cards in that suit. This means that when four cards are all you hold, once you have bid the suit there is nothing more to say about it. Only when you hold more than four cards is there something still to tell partner. When you rebid the suit you are 'saying' to partner: 'When I opened I might only have held four, but in fact I hold more than that'. We call such a suit *rebiddable*. So when you hold a reasonable five card suit there is always a rebid, if only of the five card suit, but when you don't there can be a problem.

A T 9
K 8 7 4
A T 6
Q J 5
9

For instance, if hand 9 is opened 1H and partner responds 1S, there is nowhere to go. The hearts are not rebiddable, there is no other suit to bid, and no more strength to show, so what we do is this. We say that 1NT is in itself a limit bid which does not require a rebid unless partner asks a question, when we have to answer. We then open hand 9 with a bid of 1NT.

A K 9
K J 8 7
A J 5
J 9 5
10

But then how do we bid hand 10, which has exactly the same shape? The points needed from partner just to make our contract on hand 9 could now produce game. Well, we have to invent a code. Open 1H, and over partner's response, rebid in NT, informing partner that although we have no extra heart length we have more points than if we'd *opened* 1NT.

At your present stage of play the point range for a one bid is 13, 14, 15, 16, 17, 18, 19, 20, 21. We break this into three equal part ranges:

L = 13, 14, 15 M = 16, 17, 18 U = 19, 20, 21

L **Open 1NT** (we are talking about balanced hands, remember) limiting the hand to the three point range shown, denying any singleton, and any five card suit unless it is so weak it is not rebiddable.

M **Open one of a suit**, and over most responses by partner **rebid NT at the lowest permissible level.**

U **Open one of a suit** as in M, but now over most responses by partner **make a jump rebid in NT.**

Each and all of these NT openings or rebids is a *limit bid*, stating that the bidder has nothing more to add in general to the description of the hand already given. No further rebid is needed unless partner asks a question, when an answer will be required. We shall meet some of the simpler questions that can be asked as we work through the book, but there will be more to meet in the future when your bridge progresses that far.

Other examples of a hand which is best opened 1NT are:

K 9 7	A K	K 7 2	K T 9 2	A T 9 7	A T 9	A T 7
J 8	K J 7	K Q J	Q J 7	K J 7	K J 8 7	K Q 7 4
A J 6 5	J 6 5	J T 5	A J	A T 5	T 6 5 2	J 5
A J 9 5	J 9 7 5 3	A J 9 3	Q J 5 3	J 9 5	A Q	A J 5 3
11	**12**	**13**	**14**	**15**	**16**	**17**

Examples of hands which should be opened with one of a suit and usually rebid in NT at the lowest permissible level are:

A T 9 7	K T 7	A 9 2	K 9 7	A K T
K 7 4	K 8 4 3	K J 4	K 8 7	K J
A T 6	A J 5	A J 6 5	A J 5	A T 6 5
A J 3	A Q 5	A J 3	A Q J 3	J 9 7 3
18	**19**	**20**	**21**	**22**

K 7	A K T 2	A T 9 7	A 9
K J 7	K 8	K Q 8 4	K Q 7
A J T 5	J T 6 5	A T	A T 2
A J 9 5	A Q J	A 9 3	Q J 9 7 3
23	**24**	**25**	**26**

Increase the point count until these hands enter U and they should be opened with one of a suit and usually jump rebid in NT.

HANDS WITH SUIT DISTRIBUTION

When you hold a five card suit, although there should rarely be a problem in having a rebid, what that rebid should be depends upon which of six combinations you hold, taking one characteristic from each of the following sets:

limited/intermediate/strongish hands

single suited/two suited hands

There are also *three* suited hands, the classic examples of which hold three four-card suits and a singleton. These occur relatively rarely, but we shall discuss them briefly at the end of this chapter.

First, a word about what we mean by two suited hands. Usually we mean a hand which is five–four (where there is a five card suit and a four card suit), five–five, six–five, or even more extreme. A four–four hand does not immediately qualify, because being 4432 it is reasonably balanced and can often be treated as a NT hand, but when most of the strength is in the two suits it has to be included. Six–four seems to qualify at first glance, but the considerably greater playing strength of the six card suit leads to its initial treatment as a single suited hand.

Remember, at any stage in the auction you can limit your hand by repeating any suit already bid by the partnership, or by bidding NT. A limit bid which some players forget is pass (although in strict bridge jargon this is a **call** only, and not a **bid**, *see* Glossary, page 172). In suit bidding, fit within the partnership is of great importance, together with the ability to communicate between the hands in play if the contract is won.

Consider the two EW deals shown below, which are not dealt from the set of cards for the chapter and are not necessarily compatible with hands in Chapter 4.

K J 9 6 5 3	8
8	K J 9 6 5 3
–	A K Q 7 3 2
A K Q 7 3 2	–
27	**28**

Between the two hands above, 27 and 28, there is no communication at all unless an A on the right of a K is not put up when an 8 is led, and without help from the opposition you would make far fewer tricks than you would expect from the high card count alone of 26, without adding on any distributional points as well. The hands below (29 and 30), however, with only twenty-three high card points, might even make a small slam in hearts.

K J 9 6 5 3	–
K J 7 3 2	T 8 6 5 4
A	K J 9 6 5 3
8	A K
29	**30**

The following are examples of single suited hands which should be opened with a bid of one of the suit:

K 2	A 7	A K T 9 7 2	K T 7
K J 7	K J 8 7 4	K 4	8
J 6 5	J T 6	A 5	A J T 6 5 2
A J 9 7 3	A 7 5	A 9 7	A J 3
31	**32**	**33**	**34**

K 9 2	A T 7	A
K J 4	K J 7 4	K 8
A	–	A J T 6
A J 9 7 5 3	A Q 9 7 5 3	A Q J 9 5 3
35	**36**	**37**

Hands 38 to 47 are examples of two suited hands which should be opened with a bid of one of a suit, with one three suited hand.

T 9	A K T 7 2	A K	A K T 7 2	2
K J 8 7 4	Q 8	7 3	–	K J 7 4 3
A J T 2	T	A T 6 5	A J T 6 5	A 5
A 9	A J 9 5 3	A J 9 7 5	A 5 3	A J 9 7 3
38 Open 1H	**39** Open 1C	**40** Open 1C	**41** Open 1S	**42** Open 1H

K T 9 7 2	A	K T 9 7	A	K T 9 7 2
K J 7 4 3	J 8 7 4	K Q 4	4	–
A J 5	A J T 6 5	A J T 6 5	A J T 6 5 2	A J T 6
–	A Q J	A	A J 7 5 3	A Q J 9
43 Open 1S	**44** Open 1D	**45** Open 1D	**46** Open 1D	**47** Open 1S

There are several characteristics to look for in these hands:

Are the suits of equal length? If so, are they touching or not?

Is one suit longer? If so, how much longer, and *where* is the shorter suit in relation to the longer one, above, or below?

'Touching' suits are CD, DH, HS, and surprisingly at first glance, SC. This last because of the *bidding* order of suits,

1C, 1D, 1H, *1S*, *2C*, 2D . . .

The 'higher' of two equal *touching* suits should be bid first, and the particular case of SC demonstrates the point clearly. **C** d h **S C** d h; if when you open 1C partner responds with hearts or diamonds you can bid your spades at the one level: 1C 1H
1S

while if you open 1S and partner responds in diamonds or hearts you have to go to the three level to show your clubs: 1S 2H
3C

Here the disadvantage shows up with your rebid, but with the other three cases it doesn't show up until partner's rebid.

Take DH as an example; D **H** s c D; if you bid diamonds first and partner responds 1S, you bid 2H. Now if partner prefers your diamonds the rebid takes you both to the three level: 1D 1S
2H 3D

But if you open 1H, when you rebid diamonds partner can give you preference to hearts without raising the level: 1H 1S
2D 2H

When the suits are not touching they will always consist of one major and one minor. Preference in this situation should be given to the major, bidding the minor at a later stage if the opportunity arises, and otherwise treating the hand as single suited. Hands 41 and 42 are examples of this. Hand 41 is opened 1S; hand 42 is opened 1H.

A K T 7 2	2
–	K J 7 4 3
A J T 6 5	A 5
A 5 3	A J 9 7 3
41	**42**

Remember, though, that the two suited hand has a great deal of extra playing strength if you can find some fit with partner, and there is obviously twice the chance of finding some if you can make an opportunity to bid both your suits.

The **three suited hands** we are about to discuss are of the four shapes: 4 4 4 1, 4 4 1 4, 4 1 4 4, 1 4 4 4 in the order ♠ ♥ ♦ ♣. Looking at the shape in hand 48 below first it is easy to see that the sensible opening bid is 1C. If partner makes the most probable reply of 1D you can rebid 1H, and then if partner rebids diamonds you either pass or bid NT. If partner's first response is in hearts or spades you raise one, while a supporting bid in clubs you can pass.

A T 9 7	A K 9 7	9	A T 9 2
K J 7 4	7	K J 7 4	K Q 7 4
5	A T 6 5	A T 6 5	A J T 5
A J 5 3	A Q 9 5	A J 9 7	J
48	**49**	**50**	**51**

Similarly with the shapes in hands 49 and 50, open with the suit below the singleton. In other words, open hand 49 with 1D and open hand 50 with 1H. Some recommend opening hand 50 with 1D, to allow partner to respond 1H, but this is fatuous. If partner has hearts your heart bid will be supported. 1C is tempting, but wrong. It is true, of course, that if partner responds in either diamonds or hearts your task is now easy, but at what cost? If partner makes the most likely response of 1S you are in an impossible position. Can you work out why?

Hand 51 is the exception. It has proved best to open 1H, not 1S, the suit below the singleton. If partner has four spades the response will be in spades unless there are five or more clubs in partner's hand. Then over your rebid of 2D partner may still bid spades, but if NT is preferred it will probably be a good enough contract.

4 Responding

Hands in this chapter can be bid opposite those in Chapter 3, except hands 27 to 30, and 55 and 66.

ADDING RANGES

For example, 13/15 + 11/12 means we are adding any one of a possible 13, 14, 15 to either 11 or 12, giving six combinations:

11+13=24,	11+14=25,	11+15=26;
12+13=25,	12+14=26,	12+15=27

giving us a range for the total of 24, 25, 26, 27. The **minimum** for the partnership range is obtained by adding the minima of the two individual ranges: 13/15, 11/12. 13 + 11 = 24. Similarly, the maximum for the partnership is given by the sum of the two individual maxima: 13/15, 11/12. 15 + 12 = 27.

We shall write this as 13/15 + 11/12 = 24/27.

Partnership maxima:

13/15 + 10–	13 + 10– = 23–
	14 + 10– = 24–
	15 + 10– = 25–

This translates into the simple statement that a maximum of 15 together with 10 or less gives 25 or less. Similarly, minima 13/15 + 13+ = 26+ reads as: a minimum of 13 together with at least another 13 is at least 26. In the text to come we shall simply write 13/15 + 10– = 25–
and 13/15 + 13+ = 26+

RESPONDING AFTER AN OPENING 1NT

Partner opens 1NT, showing: 13–15 points
no singleton or void
no good five card suit.

Your hand is either balanced or suit-orientated.

When your hand is balanced:

count game = 26+ partner = **1NT** = 13/15,			
26 subtract			(13/15) = (13/11)
			partner you
giving 'markers' for you of	13+	11+	10–
	13+	11/12	10–
	(b)	(c)	(a)

	Partner	You	Partnership	
(a)	13/**15**	10–	25–	There is no game.
(b)	**13**/15	13+	26+	There is a game.

There is no Game; You Pass

Let's look at an example;

Partner	**You**
A T 7	Q J 6
K Q 7 4	T 9 5
J 5	K 9 7 4
A J 5 3	K 6 2
17	**52**

Hand 17 was given on page 21 as one on which you should open, with a bid of **1NT.** Suppose partner has it and opens **1NT** when you hold hand 52. How many tricks are you sure of making? All you can guarantee are two tricks in spades, two in hearts, and two in clubs, on twenty-four points between you! True, most times you will make more, for you will not often run into the worst possible distribution and the best possible defence, but there is a long way to go from six tricks certain to nine tricks for game. So you see why we tell you to pass.

There is a Game; You Bid It

Partner	You	
K T 9 2	Q J 6	
Q J 7	A T 5	
A J	K 9 7 3	
Q J 5 3	K T 4	
14	**53**	(see page 28)

Hand 14 was given on page 21 as one on which you should open 1NT. Suppose partner has it and opens 1NT when you hold hand 53. Let's look at the tricks you should make this time. Between the two hands you have the suit combinations shown below. For instance, when 14 plays ♠2, 51 plays ♠Q, so ♠2=♠Q,

K Q J T
A Q J (T)
A K J 9
K Q J T

The spade suit must yield three tricks since the KQJT can only be beaten once by the A. There are two heart tricks, because after the ♥A the QJ can only be beaten once by the K. Since the ♥T is also held the ♥Q can be played and run if the ♥K doesn't cover (a finesse, remember), while if the K does cover on the left and you take with the A (that is QKA gone in one trick), the JT are good, so there may be three heart tricks. There are two, three, or four diamond tricks, depending upon whether the ♦Q is in a two card holding and drops, or whether it can be finessed successfully through the AJ, and upon whether the ♦T is in a three card holding and drops on AKJ, leaving the ♦9 good. There are three certain club tricks, as with the spades. This is a minimum of 3+2+2+3=10 tricks if everything is wrong, and a maximum of 3+3+4+3=13 if everything is right, although you will be highly unlikely to make twelve, let alone thirteen, for that would need the opposition to go to bed with an ace! Expect eleven tricks in such a situation. Learn to 'see' joint holdings like this prior to plotting the play.

(c) Remember our calculation:

	Game	Partner	You	Partnership	
(a)	26+	13/15	10–	25–	There is no game.
(b)		13/15	13+	26+	There is a game.

So, ten or less means no problem; thirteen or more, no problem. That leaves (c) in between, 11/12, when you don't know; as in hand 54 below.

Q 8 4 3
A T
Q 7 4 3
K T 6
54

Partner may hold:

13 or a poor 14	13(p14)	24, 25, (p26)	No game likely.
15 or a good 14	(g14)15	(g25), 26, 27	Game likely.

and you don't know which . . . but partner does, so you let partner choose. **Bid 2NT**, also in between as it were, leaving the final decision to partner.

Before you start thinking of a slam in NT you need a partnership total of 34 points, leaving 6 points = 2K = A+Q for the opposition, and even then you may not make one. Count 34–13/15 = 21/19. We deal with this situation in Chapter 7. To summarise:

Partner	*balanced*		13–15		Opens 1NT
You	*balanced*	10–	11/12	13+	
		no	maybe	yes	
	respond	pass	2NT	3NT	

The Choice Between NT and a Suit Contract

We have already indicated that there is advantage in fit between the hands, and we now wish to stress the importance of it; the hallmark of **good bidding is the successful detection of such fit.** Thirteen cards in a suit cannot divide equally, the most balanced split between the partnerships is 7, 6. Then come the other possible combinations of 8, 5; 9, 4; 10, 3 and so on. Once you have 8 to the opponents' 5 in a major suit it is likely that the major suit contract is the best one on the hand. More often than not the outstanding cards will split 3, 2; you are likely to be 5, 3 or 4, 4. **Draw trumps**; that is, in this case, taking 3 from each holding.

You		Opponents	
5, 3 (5–**3**=*2*	3–**3**=0;	3–**3**=0	2–**3** discard)
4, 4 (4–**3**=*1*	4–**3**=*1;*	3–**3**=0	2–**3** discard)

Either way you are left with two *ruffs.* Once you have nine cards in the suit between you it becomes very powerful indeed.

5, 4 v 2, 2 (5–**2**=*3* 4–**2**=*2*; 2–**2**=0 2–**2**=0) is the best of course,
but 5, 4 v 3, 1 (5–**3**=*2* 4–**3**=*1*; 3–**3**=0 1–**3**=2 discards) still gives you three ruffs.

We leave you to work out 6, 3 v 2, 2 and the other possible combinations.

There is not only the matter of extra tricks to be made in ruffs, for 4, 4 v 3, 2 leaves you 1 + 1, and if you make three tricks drawing trumps and then two ruffs, this is 3+1+1=5, one more than four tricks in the suit in NT, and that only balances the extra trick you have to make for game.

There is always the advantage of your control over opponents' long suits. **Assessment of advantage**: with eight trumps only, add points for ruffing biases, –; for each known trump over eight add one point.

Your First Conventional Bid: Stayman

A K T 2	J 5	Q 8 6 3	Q 8 4
K 8 7 4	A T 9	A T 9	A T 9 5
A T	K Q 7 3	K Q 8 4	K Q 9 3
9 7 5	K T 8 4	K T	K 8
55	**56**	**57**	**58**

So, you pick up hand 55 (dealt from the card set used in Chapter 3) and bid **1NT**. If partner has hand 56 the best contract will be 3NT, but if partner has either 57, with the partnership holding eight spades, or 58, with the partnership holding eight hearts, the best contract will be four of the relevant major. How are you to know? Sam Stayman converted the use of the bid of **2C**. When you use his bid, that is, when you 'play Stayman' 2C **is no longer natural**. Partner **alerts** (*see* Glossary). 2C no longer says 'Partner, I hold clubs'. It has become an *asking* bid. It asks partner **'have you a four card major suit?'** Partner says yes or no as follows:

Yes 2H = 'I have four hearts, I may or may not have four spades'
2S = 'I do not have four hearts or I would have bid **2H**; I *do* have four spades';

No 2D = 'I have neither four hearts nor four spades'. Partner **alerts**.
Note that 2D is now not natural, there is no statement about diamonds, only about hearts and spades.

55	**56**	**55**	**57**	**55**	**58**
1NT	3NT	1NT	**2C**	1NT	**2C**

So using Stayman the bidding sequences would have started as shown.
Hand 56 has no four card major, therefore no interest in Stayman.
Hand 57 **wants to know** if opener has four **spades**, uses **Stayman**.
Hand 58 **wants to know** if opener has four **hearts**, uses **Stayman**.

The Intermediate Hand with a Four Card Major

Q 8 4 3
A T
Q 7 4 3
K T 6
54

Now you have this tool, when you have a hand on which you wish to invite partner to bid game, and the hand contains a four card major, start by bidding **2C**. Look at hand 54 again. You have enough for game if partner is upper range for the 1NT opening, but not otherwise. But then again, should the game or part score be played in spades or NT? Well, if you start with a response of **2C**, you can find out, as we shall show you in the chapter on rebids.

When Your Hand Contains one or more Long Suits

There are, essentially, three situations. You sit opposite partner's **1NT** with:

a weakish hand which will play better in a suit;
a hand which must be played at game level or above;
an intermediate hand which may produce a game if partner either has a maximum or has fit.

As with the balanced hand, it is easier to deal with the intermediate case last; cut off the top and the bottom, then see what's left.

The Weakish Hand which will Play Better in a Suit

8 6 4 3	8 3
T 9 6 5	A 5
K 9 3	Q 9 8 7 4 3
K 8	T 8 4
59	**60**

A K	A T 9
K J 7	K J 8 7
J 6 5	T 6 5 2
J 9 7 6 3	A Q
12	**16**

Consider hands 59 and 60. They both score six high card points. When partner opens **1NT** you count: 13/15 + 6 = 19/21. The partnership has already reached its limit. Hand **59** passes. But if you count 2 points for ruffing values, played in diamonds hand 60 is worth 8 points, and may well bring home a better result played in **2D**. If that is your opinion, bid it. When there is a matter of opinion like this to be settled, the only accurate way is to compile a set of statistics. To see how to do this consider hands 12 and 16.

Played in **1NT** opposite hand 60 with a likely spade lead, hand 12 could be a disaster, losing three or more spade tricks, two or three diamond tricks, and three club tricks; eight or more tricks, two or more off. But played in **2D** there are no spade or heart losers, two or three trump losers, and three club losers. Either a made contract, or at the worst, one off. Clearly better.

Hand 16 v 60 has a better chance of seven tricks in NT, it is true, but **2D** is safe as well. So, on these hands you can't lose and may well gain by the **weak take out**. You really need to go through many more hands than this to reach a sound conclusion, but there is an inference already.

The situation becomes clearer if you have an even weaker hand. The bid of two of a suit then produces a greater improvement, for **1NT** now rarely makes, and can go off a packet, while two of a suit may make, and when it goes off is not so often a disaster.

A K	J 8 6 5 4 3	A T 9
K J 7	9 2	K J 8 7
J 6 5	9 7 4	T 6 5 2
J 9 7 6 3	6 4	A Q
12	**61**	**16**

Assess your chances with hand 61 opposite hands 12 and 16 in both the contracts 1NT and 2S. Now try laying out each pair of hands in turn and dealing the remaining twenty-six cards several times, seeing how it looks as if the deals might play. Tabulate the results and form a conclusion.

Note, however, that if you are playing Stayman **you can no longer bid 2C as a weak take out** if clubs is your suit, for partner will suppose you are asking for a four card major, and **will not pass**. This is the price you pay for the convention. If you want to keep the weak 2C take out you have to abandon Stayman. You can't have it both ways.

If you have as many as seven or eight clubs and a bust there is a way. Bid 2C, which partner in all innocence will treat as Stayman, but then over partner's rebid of 2D, 2H, or 2S, rebid your clubs, and all becomes clear.

This is a vital point to seize hold of. Once any bid becomes conventional it can no longer be used for its natural meaning. Either/or; you can't have your cake and eat it. In gaining one bid you lose another. So before introducing any conventional bid you always have to prove that it is worth giving up the original meaning; another statistical exercise, except that in the case of Stayman the homework has been done very convincingly by others before you. It is only the one bid out of four; 2D, 2H and 2S are still weak takeouts.

The Hand which should be Played at Game Level or Above

If your hand is based on a major, requiring one more trick than NT for game:

If you are sure that the game should be in the major, **bid it, 4H** or **4S.**

If you don't know whether **4H** or **4S** is better than 3NT or not, **bid 3H, 3S** whichever, and **let partner choose.**

In the latter case, partner will know you have five of the major, because if you had four you would have used Stayman and you haven't; and if you had six or more you would have bid game, and you haven't. So, holding three or more hearts or spades, partner bids **4H** or **4S**, but with two bids 3NT.

If your hand is based on a minor, a suit game requires two more tricks than NT.

Once you are committed to eleven tricks you are nearly at a slam, so in most cases the game is played in 3NT. The choice is a much clearer either/or, the minor game only being chosen on a very distributional hand.

Note: When you bid 3C, 3D, 3H, or 3S directly over partner's 1NT you are committing the partnership to a game at least. So let's look at some examples.

Q 8 6 5 4 3
A 5
Q 7 4
K T
62

Count: partner has 13/15. You have a high card count of 11, only enough for a try if your hand was balanced, but playing in spades you have – – bias, worth two points in a spade contract, and 11+2=13 which, added to partner, is enough for game **if there is a fit.** But partner at the worst will have two spades, and may have more. Bid **4S**. You may be unlucky, and find **4S** unmakeable and **3NT** on, but the odds are in your favour. This is a minimum hand for the bid.

Q 6 5
A T 9 5 2
K Q 7
K 4
63

Count: partner has 13/15. You have 14. There should be ample for game, but which should it be, 4H or 3NT? Bid 3H and let partner choose. You are guaranteeing five hearts, so partner with a three or four card fit will bid 4H, but with only two will bid 3NT.

Q J
A 9 2
K 9 8 7 4 3
K T
64

Hand 64 is best bid 3NT, because 5D needs two more tricks and only scores the same points as 3NT, while there is little likelihood of a slam.

–	T 9
A 9	K J 7 4
K Q 9 8 7 4 3	A J 6
K T 8 6	A J 9 7
65	**66**

Hand 65 is the one which is going to be played in the minor, but now there is the problem of whether you should be playing in a game or a slam. Count: twelve high card points, and if the hand is played in diamonds the D+(++), S– – –, H– bias would make it worth 17/19 points, depending on what degree of fit there is with partner. Partner's 13/15 then gives a total of 30/34, and you have to decide whether simply to bid 5D, or whether to invite partner to a slam by bidding 3D. After all, partner might have opened on hand 66.

The Intermediate Hand which may Produce Game if Partner either has a Maximum or has Fit with your Suit

Partner has opened 1NT. Our 2H says shut up, this is the contract.
Our 3H says there is at least a game on.

So how, if we have a hand with a heart suit, for instance, which is near to game but not quite there, can we say 'maybe'? Remember – like when we bid 2NT over 1NT.

The thing to do is to 'cheat'. We bid a Stayman 2C first, when holding hand 67, say, like this:

1NT	2C	1NT	2C	1NT	2C
2D	3H	2H	4H	2S	3H

8 6
A T 9 6 2
K 9 7
K T 8
67

and then bid our hearts at the three or four level, according to whether there is already fit or not. In the particular example of hand 67, 2NT would be a better rebid over partner's 2S. This is not really cheating, because any 'system' we use has to be declared to opponents.

The same method can be used if your holding is in spades or diamonds, *but not in clubs*. This is because we used 2C followed by 3C as a weak take out. You are at liberty to decide the other way about, but you can't do both.

PARTNER OPENS WITH ONE OF A SUIT

We need to remember what was said in Chapter 3, page 22. When partner opened 1NT we knew the limits of the hand, because there was only a three point range for partner's bid, but now . . .

Partner may have any one of twelve combinations, taking one characteristic from each of the two sets:

limited / **intermediate** / **strongish** hands

and **balanced** / **single suited** / **two suited** / **three suited** hands

while the high card point holding may be anything from eleven to twenty-one. So with this in mind let us look at the hands we met responding to an opening bid of 1NT, as well as some others.

Remember, partner may be sitting on twenty-one points, and then six may be enough for game, so holding six you must try to find a response. 0 to 5, then, is the lowest segment of your range. Remember, too, what we told you about fit between the hands. On page 29 we told you to respond 2NT holding a balanced 11/12 points. That holds good in principle here, and gives us another landmark. That leaves a range between 6 and 11/12. You will be ill-advised to bid at the two level without nine points or a fit with partner. Partner may have as little as eleven points and a six card suit, twelve points and a five card suit, or thirteen points.

With your 9 the partnership total is then 20/21/22, and to be at the two level on less would be foolish indeed without fit between the hands. This sometimes means that we have to bid 1NT on a hand which is not balanced.

So, 0/5; 6/(p9); (g9)/10; 11/12; 13+ are our 'landmarks'. You have, essentially, to give the most accurate, economical description of your hand.

Less than Six Points

First, then, the hand with less than six points. In this section high card point(s) is abbreviated HCP.

You hold:	When partner opens:	You respond:
J 8 6 5 4 3	1C, 1D or 1H	Pass.
9 2	1S	Pass; we know it's tempting, but if you respond with 2S partner may well go on for the wrong reasons.
9 7 4		
6 4		
61 (1HCP)		

Even if you add four for S++, H–, C– you are only worth 5 points. You can always support partner later.

The Range 6 to (p9)

When the hand is a little stronger, and the distributional values take you to 6 points, then you can give partner the simple raise, but not with less.

You hold:	When partner opens:	You respond:
8 6 4 3	1C, 1D	1H; your cheapest four card suit.
T 9 6 5	1H	2H; C– makes you worth 7 points with the fit.
K 9 3		
K 8	1S	2S; as above.
59 (6HCP)		

You hold:	When partner opens:	You respond:
8 3	1C	1D.
A 5	1D	3D; with the diamond fit your hand is now worth 6+(D++)+(S–)+(H–) = 10 points.
Q 9 8 7 4 3		
T 8 4		
60 (6HCP)	1H, 1S	1NT; we warned you.

You hold:	When partner opens:	You respond:
J 3	1C	1D.
A 5	1D	3D; either ♠J is useful because it will help develop a trick in the suit, or S– is because it won't; not both. There is a 10 card diamond fit; 8+(D++)+(H–) = 11.
K 9 8 7 4 3		
T 8 4		
68 (8HCP)		
	1H, 1S	1NT; just; with the ♦J instead of the ♦9 you would bid 2D.

You hold:	When partner opens:	You respond:
Q J 6	1C	1D.
T 9 5	1D	2D.
K 9 7 4	1H, 1S	1NT.
K 6 2		
52 (9HCP)		

You hold:	When partner opens:	You respond:
8 6	1C, 1D	1H.
A 9 6 5 2	1H	2H; even with H+, S– it is only worth 9.
K 9 7		
T 8 6	1S	1NT; don't say 2H, partner will put you with too much.
69 (7HCP)		

The Range (g9)/10

You hold:	When partner opens:	You respond:
8 6	1C, 1D	1H.
A T 9 6 2	1H	4H; H+, S–; there is nothing wasted as there was in the doubleton spade honour we met earlier; also 8's 9's and T's.
K 9 7		
K T 8		
67 (10HCP)		
	1S	2H.

You hold:	When partner opens:	You respond:
Q J 8 6 5 3	1C, 1D, 1H	1S.
A 2	1S	4S; S++, H–, D– makes you worth 14.
7 3		
K T 8		
70 (10HCP)		

You hold:	When partner opens:	You respond:
Q 8	1C	3C; the ♠Q, or S–, not both; as in hand 68.
A T 5		9+(C++)+(D–) = 12
9 3		(S–)+7+(C++)+(D–) = 11
K T 8 6 4 2		
71 (9HCP)	1D, 1H, 1S	2C.

The Range 11/12

You hold:	When partner opens:	You respond:
Q 8 4 3	1C, 1D, 1H	1S. You don't bid 2NT yet, you might miss a spade fit if you do.
A T		
Q 7 4 3		
K T 6	1S	3S; it is only a four four spade fit; 11+(H–) = 12.
54 (11HCP)		

You hold:	When partner opens:	You respond:
Q 8 4	1C, 1D	1H. You don't bid 2NT yet; why? Well, see page 38.
A T 9 5		
K Q 7	1H	3H. A major suit fit, but you have no ruffing values; the hand is only worth its 11.
8 4 2		
72 (11HCP)		
	1S	2NT. 2H would promise a five card suit.

The reason for the bidding in the above example is that on the principle of economy, if you had another four card suit of lower rank, you would have bid it; ergo, you haven't. But what if partner has four hearts as well? Partner will rebid them in the next round of bidding if partner's hand is unbalanced or if partner wants to go on, and if not you may as well play at the two level. You have no ruffing values.

You hold:	When partner opens:	You respond:
Q J 6	1C, 1H, 1S	2NT.
A 9 6	1D	2NT; there are no ruffing values, and it is a minor suit fit.
Q 8 7 3		
K 8 2		
73 (12HCP)		

You hold:	When partner opens:	You respond:
Q 8 6 5 4 3	1C, 1D, 1H	1S.
A 5	1S	4S; S++, H–, C– makes you worth 15 points.
Q 7 4		
K T		
62 (11HCP)		

You hold:	When partner opens:	You respond:
J 6 5 4 3	1C, 1D ,1H	1S; but not handled as hand 62 later in the bidding. *See* Chapter 5.
A T 5		
K 7		
K T 8	1S	4S; although not quite so good for it as hand 62. If it goes off, or if 3NT is better, bad luck.
74 (11HCP)		

You hold:	When partner opens:	You respond:
Q J 8	1C	1H; note the initial misfit and be careful.
A T 9 6 5 2		
K Q 9	1D	1H; much more optimistic though.
6	1H	There could be a slam on, *see* Chapter 5.
75 (12HCP)		
	1S	2H; again optimistic.

You hold:	When partner opens:	You respond:
Q J 8 5	1C	1S; there is a ten card club fit at least, so *if you play in clubs,* with (C++)+(H---) you are worth 16; there may be a slam on; meanwhile you look to see if there is a major suit fit as well, partly to explore the slam possibility, but also to see if there is a more lucrative contract.
–		
K Q 8		
K T 8 6 4 2		
76 (11HCP)		
	1D	2C; with the degree of fit you can afford to show the spades later.
	1H	2C; care is needed now; why?
	1S	4S; although you may respond 2C to see if a slam situation exists; *see* Chapter 5.

The Range 13+

You hold:	When partner opens:	You respond:
Q J 6	1C, 1D, 1H, 1S	3NT; there is no major suit to seek fit for.
A T 5		
K 9 7 3		
K T 4		
53 (13HCP)		

You hold:	When partner opens:	You respond:
J 5 A T 9 K Q 7 3 K T 8 4	1C	1D; there is plenty of time, and if partner has no spades you do not want to be in NT; nor do you want to miss it.
56 (13HCP)	1D	2C; as above.
	1H	2C. The cheapest *four card* suit, remember.
	1S	3NT.

You hold:	When partner opens:	You respond:
Q 8 6 3 A T 9 K Q 8 4	1C	1D; plenty of time, and if there is a slam we need to get everything right.
K T	1D, 1H	1S.
57 (14HCP)	1S	4S.

You hold:	When partner opens:	You respond:
– A 9 K Q 9 8 7 4 3 K T 8 6 **65** (12HCP)	1C	2D; could well be a slam on; a strong bid now sets the scene and gives time to look; a jump response in a new suit is *forcing* to at least game.
	1D	2C; You have 11 diamonds at least; it will need little right to make a slam; it is not easy to locate precise cards, so with D+++, S–––, H– making you worth 19 points you should maybe shoot 6D direct; on the other hand the 2C bid gives you a chance to find out more about partner's hand; the disadvantage is that opponents have plenty of time, too, to announce major suit holdings.
	1H	2D.
	1S	2D; there may be a misfit, be careful.

You hold:	When partner opens:	You respond:
Q J	1C	1D.
A 9 2	1D	5D; ♠Q J is not worth 3 points until partner has shown spade interest, and not S– as well, remember; even so, the chance of a slam makes this a better bid than 3NT.
K 9 8 7 4 3		
K T		
64 (13HCP)		
	1H, 1S	2D.

You hold:	When partner opens:	You respond:
Q 6 5	1C, 1D	1H; there is plenty of time; partner will give a valuable guide on the rebid.
A T 9 5 2		
K Q 7		
K 4	1H	4H.
63 (14HCP)	1S	2H.

You hold:	When partner opens:	You respond:
Q 8	1C	2D. With the fit already found in clubs – remember, the jump response – what does it mean?
A		
K Q 8 7 4		
K 8 6 4 2	1D	2C. Your clubs are not good enough for a jump response; the diamond suit is only just good enough for the bid above. You need at least two of the top three honours.
77 (14HCP)		
	1H, 1S	2D. Higher ranking of two five card suits; note that although in this case it looks the same as the higher of two touching suits as in openings, by this rule spades would be bid in response before clubs.

Compare the bidding for hands 68 on page 37 and 56 on page 41 with that on hand 77 above. When you are bidding four card suits you need four from partner to give a sufficient fit to play with the suit as trumps. When you have a five card suit you need less from partner. When you rebid clubs after diamonds with hand 77, partner knows you have at least five diamonds. With the other hands, when partner does not bid your other four card suit you are prepared to conceal it.

5 Rebids: The Complete Uncontested Bidding Sequence

Note: The NT type hand which is intially too strong to open 1NT. If it is 4, 3, 3, 3 of any kind there is no problem; you open the four card suit. When it is 4, 4, 3, 2 of some kind there are various arguments for particular bid selections, and there is not complete agreement among all players as to what the results of those arguments are, so for now let's keep it simple. With one exception, we recommend you to bid the higher ranking suit. The exception is when you have spades and hearts; in this case open 1H. This matches the 4, 4, 4, 1 distribution where the singleton is a club, discussed on page 25.

In this chapter we shall list all the responsive hands from the last chapter which lead to a rebid from opener, and consider various hands opener might have had, examining the way the bidding should vary with circumstance. While doing this we shall take the hands in numerical order, rather than in the logical sequence they were dealt with in Chapter 4. This will cause them to arrive more at random, as they do in fact at the bridge table. If you wish to look up something particular, turn to the appendix of hands (page 163), which you can use to trace your problem. Look through it for a hand similar to the one which has caused your problem, and turn to the various pages where the hand is listed as appearing.

We shall not pretend that every hand lends itself to perfect treatment. Time after time at the bridge table situations arise where you list your possible replies, and none of them tells the truth. But remember, we spoke of developing judgement. The art lies in selecting the most effective lie (or the least damaging).

HAND 52

On page 27 hand 52, with nine points, passed partner's 1NT. Now it has to respond. It also appears on page 37.

K 9 2	Q J 6	A K 9 7	Q J 6	K T 9 7	Q J 6
K J 4	T 9 5	7	T 9 5	K J 8743	T 9 5
A	K 9 7 4	A T 6 5	K 9 7 4	A J	K 9 7 4
A J 9753	K 6 2	A Q 9 5	K 6 2	7	K 6 2
35	**52**	**49**	**52**	**79**	**52**

1C	1D	1D	2D	1H	1NT
(a)1NT	2NT(b)	2S	3S(d)	2H	P
(c)3NT	P	4C	5D		
		P			

A K 9 7 2	Q J 6	A 9	Q J 6	K 9	Q J 6
K J 8	T 9 5	K Q 7	T 9 5	K J 7 4	T 9 5
J 6	K 9 7 4	A T 2	K 9 7 4	A J T 652	K 9 7 4
A J 7	K 6 2	Q J 973	K 6 2	7	K 6 2
78	**52**	**26**	**52**	**80**	**52**

1S	1NT	1C	1D	1D	2D
(e)2NT	3NT(b)	1NT	2NT(b)	P	
P		P			

K T 7	Q J 6	A K T 2	Q J 6
K 8 4 3	T 9 5	K 8	T 9 5
A J 5	K 9 7 4	J T 6 5	K 9 7 4
A Q 5	K 6 2	A Q J	K 6 2
19	**52**	**24**	**52**

1H	1NT	1S	1NT
(e)P		2NT	3NT(b)
		P	

(a) The hand is too good for a mere **2C**, and now that partner has shown cover for diamonds **1NT** becomes the best bid.
(b) The original bid required six points; you have nine.
(c) The potential of the club suit makes the hand better than minimum.
(d) Partner will know there are only three cards; you didn't reply **1S** earlier.

(e) Partner possibly 6, 7, 8 or 9; you need 9; odds of 3 to 1 against; the flat hand 19 isn't worth it, but the extra spade length in hand 78 tips the scale.

HAND 53

On page 27 hand 53, with thirteen points, raised partner's **1NT** to three. It also appears on page 40.

A	Q J 6
K 8	A T 5
A J T 6	K 9 7 3
A Q J 9 5 3	K T 4
37	**53**

1C 3NT
(a)6C P

K T 9 7	Q J 6
K Q 4	A T 5
A J T 6 5	K 9 7 3
A	K T 4
45	**53**

1D 3NT
(b)P

A T 9 7	Q J 6
K Q 8 4	A T 5
A T	K 9 7 3
A 9 3	K T 4
25	**53**

1H 3NT
(b)P

A T 9 7	Q J 6
K 7 4	A T 5
A T 6	K 9 7 3
A J 3	K T 4
18	**53**

1S 3NT
P

K T 7	Q J 6
8	A T 5
A J T 6 5 2	K 9 7 3
A J 3	K T 4
34	**53**

1D 3NT
5D P

A K T 7 2	Q J 6
–	A T 5
A J T 6 5	K 9 7 3
A 5 3	K T 4
41	**53**

1S 3NT
4D 5D(d)
6D P

K T 9 7	Q J 6
K J 8 7 4 3	A T 5
A J	K 9 7 3
7	K T 4
79	**53**

1H 3NT
(c)4H P

(a) Partner does not have four spades or hearts, or five diamonds, or they would have been bid, so partner has at most three hearts, three spades, and four diamonds, and so at least three clubs, giving at least nine trumps.

(b) There is no need to waste time looking for a spade fit; if partner had four spades, they would have been bid.
(c) There is no need to waste time looking for a spade fit; then again, partner will have at least two hearts for the **3NT** bid, which means at least eight trumps.
(d) Partner may have only four diamonds, but then the spades will be worth discards, although **4S** is worth more points than **5D** for fewer tricks; however, there might be a slam on, and **5D** sounds more encouraging; after all, the spade and diamond holdings are not at all bad.

HAND 54

On page 28 we told you to bid **2NT** on hand 54, and then on page 31, after we had introduced you to Stayman (2C, remember) we recommended a 'look see' on the way. It also appears on page 38.

K T 9 2	Q 8 4 3	A T 9 7	Q 8 4 3	A T 7 2	Q 8 4 3
Q J 7	A T	K J 7	A T	K J 8 7	A T
A J	Q 7 4 3	A T 5	Q 7 4 3	A 6	Q 7 4 3
Q J 5 3	K T 6	J 9 5	K T 6	J 9 5	K T 6
14	**54**	**15**	**54**	**81**	**54**

1NT	2C(a)	1NT	2C(a)	1NT	2C(a)
(b)2S	3S(c)	(b)2S	3S(c)	(f)2H	2NT(g)
(d)4S	P	(e)P		(h)3S	P

A K T 2	Q 8 4 3	A K	Q 8 4 3	A T 9	Q 8 4 3
K 8 7 4	A T	K J 7	A T	K J 8 7	A T
A T	Q 7 4 3	J 6 5	Q 7 4 3	T 6 5 2	Q 7 4 3
9 7 5	K T 6	J 9 7 5 3	K T 6	A Q	K T 6
55	**54**	**12**	**54**	**16**	**54**

1NT	2C(a)	1NT	2C(a)	1NT	2C(a)
(f)2H	2NT(g)	(j)2D	2NT(k)	(f)2H	2NT(g)
(i)4S	P	(e)P		(m)P	

(a) Have you a four card major, partner?
(b) Yes, I have four spades but not four hearts.
(c) So have I, with 11/12 points.
(d) I am not minimum, so let's have a go.
(e) So what.

(f) Yes, I have four hearts; I may or may not have four spades.
(g) I haven't, but I do have four spades and 11/12 points.
(h) I have four spades too, but cannot go any further.
(i) I have four spades too, and am not minimum; let's have a go.
(j) No.
(k) I have, and I have 11/12 points.
(m) Nearly, but the ♣AQ looks very vulnerable . . .

K 9 7	Q 8 4 3
K 8 7	A T
A J 5	Q 7 4 3
A Q J 3	K T 6
21	**54**

1C	1S(a)
(b)1NT	3NT
P	

K 9 2	Q 8 4 3
K J 4	A T
A	Q 7 4 3
A J 9 7 5 3	K T 6
35	**54**

1C	1S(a)
(c)3C	3NT(d)
P	

A	Q 8 4 3
4	A T
A J T 6 5 2	Q 7 4 3
A J 7 5 3	K T 6
46	**54**

1D	1S(e)
2C	3D(f)
(g)4C	4H(g)
(g)4S	5C(h)
6D	P

A K 9 7	Q 8 4 3
7	A T
A T 6 5	Q 7 4 3
A Q 9 5	K T 6
49	**54**

1D	1S(e)
(i)3S	4S(j)
P	

(a) If the hand had any immediate slam interest 1D would be better, giving partner as much detail as possible on which to base a final decision.
(b) I have a NT type hand of sixteen to eighteen points.
(c) Although the club suit could be better, with the semi spade fit, and the shortage in diamonds, this is the best bid available.
(d) With the other two suits stopped, this is likely to be easier than 5C for the same score.
(e) There might also be a spade fit, which would score more.
(f) The hand begins to look very good indeed; pass on the good news with **a jump rebid.**
(g) **Cue bids** (*see* Glossary and the chapter on slam bidding) showing the A.

(h) Partner has shown the ♣A, so this is a cue bid showing the ♣K.
(i) There is!
(j) My 1S bid could have been made on six or seven points . . .

A 7	Q 8 4 3	K T 9 7	Q 8 4 3	A K T 9 7 2	Q 8 4 3
K J 8 7 4	A T	K J 8 7 4 3	A T	K 4	A T
J T 6	Q 7 4 3	A J	Q 7 4 3	A 5	Q 7 4 3
A 7 5	K T 6	7	K T 6	A 9 7	K T 6
32	**54**	**79**	**54**	**33**	**54**

1H	1S(a)	1H	1S(a)	1S	3S(f)
2H	2NT(b)	(d)2S	2NT(e)	(g)5S	6S
(c)3NT	P	4S	P	P	

A K T 7 2	Q 8 4 3
–	A T
A J T 6 5	Q 7 4 3
A 5 3	K T 6
41	**54**

1S	3S(f)
(h)5D	5H(i)
5S	6S(j)
P	

(a) There may be a spade fit, and this is the best way to find out.
(b) I have eleven or twelve points, but looked for a spade fit first.
(c) Thirteen high card points, and five hearts already shown.
(d) There is!
(e) Show partner my eleven points and leave all the options open . . .
(f) With six or seven points you would have to bid 2S, while you need thirteen to be worth game.
(g) Invitational; asks partner to bid six if a maximum.
(h) The jump shows both strength and a second suit.
(i) A cue bid showing the A.
(j) Partner doesn't know about the diamond fit, but I do.

HAND 56

On page 30 hand 56 raised partner's opening 1NT to three. It also appears on page 41.

K 2	J 5	A K T	J 5
K J 7	A T 9	K J	A T 9
J 6 5	K Q 7 3	A T 6 5	K Q 7 3
A J 9 7 3	K T 8 4	J 9 7 3	K T 8 4
31	**56**	**22**	**56**

1C	1D(a)	1D	2C(a)
2C	4C(b)	2NT	3D(d)
(c)P		(e)3S	3NT(f)(a+)

(a) Yes, we know about the club fit in the one case and the diamond fit in the other, but there may be a NT contract which will be more lucrative for fewer tricks.
(a+) See what we mean?
(b) Partner has thirteen to fifteen, with five or more clubs; say thirteen, and five; that will be nine trumps when we play in clubs, which will allow one point to be added for my doubleton spade, but then I have to disallow the point for the ♠J; quits; but I can still add one for the ninth trump; 13+13+1=27. Do you remember the table of expectation on page 16? If so, you'll know that you need twenty-nine to thirty to expect eleven tricks on balanced hands; if you had balanced hands your 13+13=26 would be enough for game, but you aren't good enough here. However, suppose partner has 15? Then partner will raise . . .
(c) I have already show partner thirteen points and five clubs, so I should really pass, although it's very tempting.
(d) I'm not too happy about NT, and I have a diamond fit I've not told you about yet which may mean there's a game or slam in diamonds.
(e) Well, there's no need to worry about spades.
(f) Oh, alright then.

T 9	J 5	A K T 7 2	J 5	A T 7	J 5
K J 8 7 4	A T 9	–	A T 9	K Q 7 4	A T 9
A J T 2	K Q 7 3	A J T 6 5	K Q 7 3	J 5	K Q 7 3
A 9	K T 8 4	A 5 3	K T 8 4	A J 5 3	K T 8 4
38	**56**	**41**	**56**	**17**	**56**

1H	2C	1S	3NT	1NT	3NT
2D	4H(g)	4D	5D(h)	P	
P		(i)6D	P		

T 9	J 5
K J 7 4	A T 9
A J 6	K Q 7 3
A J 9 7	K T 8 4
66	**56**

1NT **3NT**(j)
P

(g) Partner is extremely likely to have five hearts, for if the hand was 4, 4 NT would either have been opened or rebid unless there is the rare 4, 4, 4, 1; 4H is therefore likely to be easier than 5D.
(h) Partner does not want to play in NT, and of the two suits shown you much prefer diamonds; so much so that it is tempting to go on; but remember – your 3NT bid showed the full value of your hand, now you may only answer questions.
(i) There must be a good play for it, while to find out if partner has the particular cards which would produce seven is impossible.
(j) This kind of thing will happen from time to time, but even when it does, opponents don't always find the right lead, especially with no suit information given to them by your bidding.

HAND 57

On page 30 hand 57 used Stayman over partner's **1NT**. It appears on page 41 also.

A T 7	Q 8 6 3	A	Q 8 6 3	9	Q 8 6 3
K J 7 4	A T 9	J 8 7 4	A T 9	K J 7 4	A T 9
–	K Q 8 4	A J T 6 5	K Q 8 4	A T 6 5	K Q 8 4
A Q 9 7 5 3	K T	A Q J	K T	A J 9 7	K T
36	**57**	**44**	**57**	**50**	**57**

1C	1D	1D	1S	1H	1S
1H	1S	(a)1NT	3D	2C	3NT
2C	3NT	(b)4C	4H(b)	P	
		(b)4S	5C(b)		
		(c)6D	P		

K T 9 7 2	Q 8 6 3	A T 9 7	Q 8 6 3	T 9	Q 8 6 3
–	A T 9	K J 7	A T 9	K J 7 4	A T 9
A J T 6	K Q 8 4	A T 5	K Q 8 4	A J 6	K Q 8 4
A Q J 9	K T	J 9 5	K T	A J 9 7	K T
47	**57**	**15**	**57**	**66**	**57**

1S	2D	1NT	2C(f)	1NT	2C(f)
4D	5S(d)	(g)2S	4S	(h)2H	3NT(i)
(e)P		P		(j)P	

(a) Partner either doesn't have four hearts, or is at least five four and will bid them over my NT; in any case, although **1NT** is not ideal, the heart suit is not good enough to reverse.
(b) Cue bids, remember?
(c) Once partner has shown at least eight cards in diamonds and spades, there are no more than five cards in clubs and hearts, and with ♥A and ♣K shown (against your ♣AQJ) four of those are covered, making the slam odds on.
(d) An invitation.
(e) The trump suit is so poor in the context of the bidding, and trump control in a slam is vital.
(f) Stayman.
(g) Yes, I have four spades.
(h) Yes, I have four hearts, I may or may not have four spades.
(i) Partner will know I have four spades.
(j) Thank goodness partner has four spades.

HAND 58

On page 30 hand 58 used Stayman over partner's 1NT.

A K T 7 2	Q 8 4	K T 7	Q 8 4	A T 9 2	Q 8 4
Q 8	A T 9 5	8	A T 9 5	K Q 7 4	A T 9 5
T	K Q 9 3	A J T 6 5 2	K Q 9 3	A J T 5	K Q 9 3
A J 9 5 3	K 8	A J 3	K 8	J	K 8
39	**58**	**34**	**58**	**51**	**58**

(a)1C	1D(b)	1D	1H(c)	1H	4H
1S	3NT	2D	3NT(d)	P	
P		P			

K T 9 7 2	Q 8 4	K 9 7	Q 8 4	A T 9	Q 8 4
K J 7 4 3	A T 9 5	J 8	A T 9 5	K J 8 7	A T 9 5
A J 5	K Q 9 3	A J 6 5	K Q 9 3	T 6 5 2	K Q 9 3
–	K 8	A J 9 5	K 8	A Q	K 8
43	**58**	**11**	**58**	**16**	**58**

1S	2D		1NT	2C(f)		1NT	2C(f)
(e)2H	4H	(g)	2D	3NT	(h)	2H	4H
P			P			P	

(a) Two 'touching' suits, remember?
(b) If partner has hearts they will be bid next.
(c) The search for a 4, 4 fit in a major suit.
(d) You will see that **6D** looks likely when you see the hands together, but bidding it is another thing; **3NT** is good enough for now.
(e) It is tempting to bid **3H** on the distribution and the diamond fit, but you just aren't good enough.
(f) Stayman.
(g) I have no four card major.
(h) Yes, I have four hearts; I may or may not have four spades.

HAND 59

On page 31 hand 59 passed partner's opening **1NT** bid. It also appears on page 36.

K 9 7	8 6 4 3	K 2	8 6 4 3	A K T 7 2	8 6 4 3
K 8 7	T 9 6 5	K J 7	T 9 6 5	Q 8	T 9 6 5
A J 5	K 9 3	J 6 5	K 9 3	T	K 9 3
A Q J 3	K 8	A J 9 7 3	K 8	A J 9 5 3	K 8
21	**59**	**31**	**59**	**39**	**59**

1C	1H	1C	1H	1C	1H
1NT	P	2C	P	1S	2S
				3S	P

AT97	8643	KT7	8643	A	8643
KJ74	T965	8	T965	J874	T965
5	K93	AJT652	K93	AJT65	K93
AJ53	K8	AJ3	K8	AQJ	K8
48	**59**	**34**	**59**	**44**	**59**

1C 1H
2H P

1D 1H
2D P

1D 1H
3H P(a)

KT7	8643	T9	8643	AT92	8643
K843	T965	KJ874	T965	KQ74	T965
AJ5	K93	AJT2	K93	AJT5	K93
AQ5	K8	A9	K8	J	K8
19	**59**	**38**	**59**	**51**	**59**

1H 2H
P

1H 2H
P

1H 2H
P

AKT9	8643	AT97	8643	AT972	8643
KJ874	T965	K74	T965	8	T965
T	K93	AT6	K93	AJT	K93
A95	K8	AJ3	K8	AJ73	K8
82	**59**	**18**	**59**	**83**	**59**

1H 2H
2S 3H(b)
P

1S 2S
P

1S 2S
3S P

(a) If partner had been a shade stronger you would be playing in game, which is why you must bid.
(b) Yes, we know you have four spades, but even though you have found a fit in two suits your contributions are as weak as they can be; you have already bid your hand to the limit on the first response.

HAND 60

On page 31 hand 60 bid 2D as a weak take out over partner's opening 1NT. *See also* page 37.

A T 7	8 3	A	8 3
K J 7 4	A 5	K 8	A 5
–	Q 9 8 7 4 3	A J T 6	Q 9 8 7 4 3
A Q 9 7 5 3	T 8 4	A Q J 9 5 3	T 8 4
36	**60**	**37**	**60**

1C	1D	1C	1D
1H	2C(a)	4D	4H(b)
P		(b)4S	5D
		6D	P

K T 9 7	8 3	K 7	8 3
K Q 4	A 5	K J 7	A 5
A J T 6 5	Q 9 8 7 4 3	A J T 5	Q 9 8 7 4 3
A	T 8 4	A J 9 5	T 8 4
45	**60**	**23**	**60**

1D	3D	1D	3D
(c)3S	4D	3NT	P
5D	P	P	

2	8 3	A T 9 7 2	8 3
K J 7 4 3	A 5	K Q 7	A 5
A 5	Q 9 8 7 4 3	6	Q 9 8 7 4 3
A J 9 7 3	T 8 4	A J 5 3	T 8 4
42	**60**	**84**	**60**

1H	1NT	1S	1NT
2C	2H(d)	2C	2S(d)
		P	

(a) Do not rebid diamonds, partner may be void; 2C is just as much a sign off.
(b) Cue bids.
(c) A try for NT.
(d) Do not rebid diamonds; partner may be void or singleton; then again, as we saw in an earlier hand, partner is almost certain to have a five card major, and may only have four of the second suit.

HAND 62

On page 33 hand 62 'shot' 4S over partner's opening 1NT.

A K	Q 8 6 5 4 3	A	Q 8 6 5 4 3
7 3	A 5	K 8	A 5
A T 6 2	Q 7 4	A J T 6	Q 7 4
A J 9 7 5	K T	A Q J 9 5 3	K T
40	**62**	**37**	**62**

1C	1S	1C	1S
(a)2D	3S	(a)2D	3S
4S	P	4C	6C(b)
		P	

K T 9 7	Q 8 6 5 4 3	A 9 2	Q 8 6 5 4 3
K Q 4	A 5	K J 4	A 5
A J T 6 5	Q 7 4	A J 6 5	Q 7 4
A	K T	A J 3	K T
45	**62**	**20**	**62**

1D	1S	1D	1S
3S	5S	1NT	4S
6S	P	P	

A T 7	Q 8 6 5 4 3	9	Q 8 6 5 4 3
K Q 7 4	A 5	K J 7 4	A 5
J 5	Q 7 4	A T 6 5	Q 7 4
A J 5 3	K T	A J 9 7	K T
17	**62**	**50**	**62**

1NT	4S	1H	1S
P		2C	3S
		P	

A 7	Q 8 6 5 4 3	A K T 2	Q 8 6 5 4 3
K J 8 7 4	A 5	K 8	A 5
J T 6	Q 7 4	J T 6 5	Q 7 4
A 7 5	K T	A Q J	K T
32	**62**	**24**	**62**

1H 1S
2H 3S

1S 4S
P

A T 9 7 2	Q 8 6 5 4 3	T 9	Q 8 6 5 4 3
8	A 5	K J 7 4	A 5
A J T	Q 7 4	A J 6	Q 7 4
A J 7 3	K T	A J 9 7	K T
83	**62**	**66**	**62**

1S 4S
P

1NT 4S
P

(a) The reverse bid is strong, remember.
(b) On the bidding the ♣K,♦Q,♥A must be gold dust, since partner has no spade interest.

HAND 63

On page 34 hand 63 responded to partner's opening 1NT with a bid of 3H. It also appears on page 42.

A 9	Q 6 5	K 9	Q 6 5
K Q 7	A T 9 5 2	K J 7 4	A T 9 5 2
A T 2	K Q 7	A J T 6 5 2	K Q 7
Q J 9 7 3	K 4	7	K 4
26	**63**	**80**	**63**

1C 1H
(a) 1NT 3H
4H P

1D 1H
2H 4H
P

A K T 9	Q 6 5
K J 8 7 4	A T 9 5 2
T	K Q 7
A 9 5	K 4
82	**63**

1H	4H
(b)4S	4NT(c)
(d)5C	6H
P	

A T 9 7	Q 6 5
K 7 4	A T 9 5 2
A T 6	K Q 7
A J 3	K 4
18	**63**

1S	2H
2NT	3S(e)
(f)4H	P

K 9 7	Q 6 5
J 8	A T 9 5 2
A J 6 5	K Q 7
A J 9 5	K 4
11	**63**

1NT	3H
3NT	P

A T 9	Q 6 5
K J 8 7	A T 9 5 2
T 6 5 2	K Q 7
A Q	K 4
16	**63**

1NT	3H
4H	P

(a) It is more important to tell partner about the point count at the moment than about the five card club suit.
(b) The hand is now worth eighteen points, and must make some try; cue bidding the ♠A will allow partner to show ♦A if it is held.
(c) Showing interest, but unable to cue bid; 5H would be a sign off.
(d) The ♣A as well.
(e) Partner may have a five card spade suit and a doubleton heart.
(f) Partner doesn't sound interested in NT, so with three card support for what must be a five card suit . . . Indeed, there was a case for bidding 4H direct on the previous round; partner had shown enough points to bid at the two level, which together with your sixteen is enough for game, and you knew there was a five three heart fit.

HAND 64

On page 34 hand 64 responded to partner's 1NT by raising to three. It also appears on page 42.

A T 9 7	Q J
K J 7 4	A 9 2
5	K 9 8 7 4 3
A J 5 3	K T
48	**64**

1C 1D
1H 3NT(a)
P

A	Q J
4	A 9 2
A J T 6 5 2	K 9 8 7 4 3
A J 7 5 3	K T
46	**64**

1D 5D
(b)6D P

A 7	Q J
K J 8 7 4	A 9 2
J T 6	K 9 8 7 4 3
A 7 5	K T
32	**64**

1H 2D
2H 4H(c)
P

A K T 9 7 2	Q J
K 4	A 9 2
A 5	K 9 8 7 4 3
A 9 7	K T
33	**64**

1S 2D
3S 4NT(d)
(e)5S 5NT(f)
(g)6H 7S(h)
P

A T 7	Q J
K Q 7 4	A 9 2
J 5	K 9 8 7 4 3
A J 5 3	K T
17	**64**

1NT 3NT
P

(a) Not an easy one; 3D is not forcing, and 4D may put you into a 5D contract with diamond losers, the suit is really poor; take a chance for now, and learn how to bid it in a more sophisticated way when your bridge is stronger.
(b) If partner doesn't have the ♥A then there must be points in diamonds and clubs.
(c) Partner now has at least five hearts, making at least eight, a viable trump suit.
(d) The ♠QJ are now very good support, so you can afford to start looking for a slam in spades; you need to know how many aces are missing, so you use a **conventional bid** called **Blackwood**; 4NT=how many aces have you, partner? *See also* Chapter 9 on slams.

(e) This bid follows 4NT=have you any aces partner?, and is 5C=0 5D=1 5H=2 5S=3, and *not* a limit bid in spades.
(f) How many kings have you, partner?
(g) 6C=0 6D=1 6H=2.
(h) Can you see where thirteen tricks are coming from? *See* Chapter 11 on play.

HAND 65

On page 34 hand 65 had a problem after partner's opening 1NT. It also appears on page 41.

A K	–
7 3	A 9
A T 6 2	K Q 9 8 7 4 3
A J 9 7 5	K T 8 6
40	**65**

	1C	2D(a)
(b)	3D	4C(c)
(d)	4S	6D
	P	

K 7	–
K J 7	A 9
A J T 5	K Q 9 8 7 4 3
A J 9 5	K T 8 6
23	**65**

	1D	2C(e)
(f)	2NT	6D
	P	

A T 9 7	–
K Q 8 4	A 9
A T	K Q 9 8 7 4 3
A 9 3	K T 8 6
25	**65**

	1H	2D
(f)	2NT	3C(g)
	3S	5D(g)
(h)	6D	P

K T 9 7 2	–
K J 7 4 3	A 9
A J 5	K Q 9 8 7 4 3
–	K T 8 6
43	**65**

1S	2D(i)
2H	4D
5D	P

K T 9 2	–
Q J 7	A 9
A J	K Q 9 8 7 4 3
Q J 5 3	K T 8 6
14	**65**

1NT 3D
3S 3NT(j)
P

(a) With the club fit already known it becomes a big enough hand for the jump shift.
(b) There is no need to jump the bidding again, partner won't pass.
(c) Showing fit in both minors.
(d) This cue bid shows hand 65 where the heart loser can go quickly if necessary.
(e) Any diamond response is limiting; the hand cannot afford this. A forcing bid has to be found; diamonds can always be confirmed later.
(f) I have a balanced/semi balanced hand of sixteen to eighteen points.
(g) A direct bid of 5D would deny interest in a slam.
(h) There are unlikely to be any wasted values.
(i) Care is needed with a potential misfit showing.
(j) With stops in clubs and hearts hand 65 prefers this to 5D, which requires two more tricks for the same score.

HAND 67

On page 35 hand 67 started with a Stayman 2C over partner's opening 1NT. It also appears on page 38.

K 9 7	8 6	A T 7	8 6
K 8 7	A T 9 6 2	K J 7 4	A T 9 6 2
A J 5	K 9 7	–	K 9 7
A Q J 3	K T 8	A Q 9 7 5 3	K T 8
21	**67**	**36**	**67**

1C	1H	1C	1H
(a) 1NT	3H(b)	3H	4H
4H	P	P	

K T 7	8 6	A 7	8 6
8	A T 9 6 2	K J 8 7 4	A T 9 6 2
A J T 6 5 2	K 9 7	J T 6	K 9 7
A J 3	K T 8	A 7 5	K T 8
34	**67**	**32**	**67**

1D	1H	1H	4H
2D	3D	P	
P			

A T 9 7 2	8 6	A K T 2	8 6
8	A T 9 6 2	K 8	A T 9 6 2
A J T	K 9 7	J T 6 5	K 9 7
A J 7 3	K T 8	A Q J	K T 8
83	**67**	**24**	**67**

1S	2H	1S	2H
2S	P(c)	2NT	3NT(d)
		P	

(a) 16–18; NT distribution, not four hearts (or I'd have raised ♥).
(b) I have at least five hearts and enough points for game, but I don't know which is best.
(c) Borderline, because there are only three cards below 7, but not quite good enough.
(d) Partner knows I have only five hearts now; if I had more I would have bid 4H.

HAND 68

On page 37 we met hand 68.

A K T 7 2	J 3	A	J 3
Q 8	A 5	J 8 7 4	A 5
T	K 9 8 7 4 3	A J T 6 5	K 9 8 7 4 3
A J 9 5 3	T 8 4	A Q J	T 8 4
39	**68**	**44**	**68**

1C	1D	1D	3D
1S	2C(a)	5D	P
P			

A T 9 2	J 3	A K T 7 2	J 3
K Q 7 4	A 5	–	A 5
A J T 5	K 9 8 7 4 3	A J T 6 5	K 9 8 7 4 3
J	T 8 4	A 5 3	T 8 4
51	**68**	**41**	**68**

1H 1NT(b)
(c)P

1S 1NT
2D 4D
6D P

A K	J 3
K J 7	A 5
J 6 5	K 9 8 7 4 3
J 9 7 5 3	T 8 4
12	**68**

1NT 2D
P

(a) Do not rebid diamonds, partner may be singleton or void; there will probably be at least five clubs in partner's hand or NT would have been opened or rebid.
(b) You are not good enough to respond at the two level, but you are too strong to pass.
(c) Partner has shown not more than nine points; there is nowhere to go; when the hand comes to be played however, there is a play for 6D! That's life . . .

HAND 69

On page 37 we met hand 69.

A	8 6	A K T	8 6
K 8	A 9 6 5 2	K J	A 9 6 5 2
A J T 6	K 9 7	A T 6 5	K 9 7
A Q J 9 5 3	T 8 6	J 9 7 3	T 8 6
37	**69**	**22**	**69**

1C 1H
(a)2D 3C
(b)3S 4H(b)
5C 6C(c)

1D 1H
1NT P(d)

T 9	8 6	A K 9 7 2	8 6
K J 8 7 4	A 9 6 5 2	K J 8	A 9 6 5 2
A J T 2	K 9 7	J 6	K 9 7
A 9	T 8 6	A J 7	T 8 6
38	**69**	**78**	**69**

1H 2H
P

1S 1NT(e)
2NT P

K 9 7	8 6	A T 7 2	8 6
J 8	A 9 6 5 2	K J 8 7	A 9 6 5 2
A J 6 5	K 9 7	A 6	K 9 7
A J 9 5	T 8 6	J 9 5	T 8 6
11	**69**	**81**	**69**

1NT 2H(f)
P

1NT 2H(f)
P

(a) The reverse shows a strong hand, remember?
(b) Cue bids.
(c) Partner doesn't know about my ♦K.
(d) Partner has 16 to 18, you have 7; total, 23 to 25.
(e) You dare not pass, yet are not strong enough to bid at the 2 level.
(f) Twenty to twenty-two between you; with a six card suit you should certainly bid 2H, but with this hand it is a matter of opinion; if you get several adverse results, think again.

HAND 70

On page 38 we met hand 70.

A 9	Q J 8 6 5 3	A	Q J 8 6 5 3
K Q 7	A 2	4	A 2
A T 2	7 3	A J T 6 5 2	7 3
Q J 9 7 3	K T 8	A J 7 5 3	K T 8
26	**70**	**46**	**70**

1C 1S
1NT 4S(a)
P

1D 1S
2C 2D(b)
(c)3C 4C
P

2	Q J 8 6 5 3	A K T 9	Q J 8 6 5 3
K J 7 4 3	A 2	K J 8 7 4	A 2
A 5	7 3	T	7 3
A J 9 7 3	K T 8	A 9 5	K T 8
42	**70**	**82**	**70**

1H	1S	1H	1S
2C	2H(b)	(d)3S	4S
P		P	

T 9	Q J 8 6 5 3	A K T 9 7 2	Q J 8 6 5 3
K J 7 4	A 2	K 4	A 2
A J 6	7 3	A 5	7 3
A J 9 7	K T 8	A 9 7	K T 8
66	**70**	**33**	**70**

1NT	2C(e)	1S	4S
2H	3S(f)	(h)6S	P
(g)P			

(a) 16–18 + 10 = 26–28, and 1NT should mean partner has at least two spades, which means eight trumps at least; add 2 = H– D–.
(b) Do not rebid your spades; partner may be singleton or void.
(c) Shows at least 5, 5 and better than minimum.
(d) Fifteen HCP, eight trumps, so D– – makes seventeen.
(e) Stayman.
(f) If I had bid 3S directly it would have been a game force; 2S now would be invitational with a five card suit; this is invitational with a six card suit.
(g) A close thing, but not quite.
(h) There is a classical bridge problem here due to **mirror distribution** (*see* Glossary); it looks at first as though you must lose one diamond and one club, but do not despair; turn to the chapter on play!

HAND 71

On page 38 we met hand 71.

A T 9 7	Q 8	K 9	Q 8
K J 7 4	A T 5	K J 7 4	A T 5
5	9 3	A J T 6 5 2	9 3
A J 5 3	K T 8 6 4 2	7	K T 8 6 4 2
48	**71**	**80**	**71**

1C 3C
(a)P

1D 2C
2D P(b)

9	Q 8	K T 9 7 2	Q 8
K J 7 4	A T 5	–	A T 5
A T 6 5	9 3	A J T 6	9 3
A J 9 7	K T 8 6 4 2	A Q J 9	K T 8 6 4 2
50	**71**	**47**	**71**

1H 2C
3C P(a)

1S 2C
4C 5C
P

A K T 2	Q 8
K 8 7 4	A T 5
A T	9 3
9 7 5	K T 8 6 4 2
55	**71**

1NT P(c)

(a) There is a very good chance of game as things turn out; in the opposite way to how 6S could fail on the last page; here, in 48v71 the diamond singleton is entirely effective, being opposite no values at all, while in 50v71 the ♦A is opposite a doubleton, leaving only one loser again.
(b) At least you have a doubleton; *do not* rebid your clubs, partner may be singleton or void.
(c) You cannot make a weak take out, remember; the price you paid for adopting Stayman.

HAND 72

On page 39 we met hand 72.

K 2	Q 8 4	A 9 2	Q 8 4	2	Q 8 4
K J 7	A T 9 5	K J 4	A T 9 5	K J 7 4 3	A T 9 5
J 6 5	K Q 7	A J 6 5	K Q 7	A 5	K Q 7
A J 9 7 3	8 4 2	A J 3	8 4 2	A J 9 7 3	8 4 2
31	**72**	**20**	**72**	**42**	**72**

1C	1H	1D	1H	1H	3H
2C	2NT(a)	(b)1NT	3NT	4H	P
P		P			

A K 9 7 2	Q 8 4	A K	Q 8 4	A T 7	Q 8 4
K J 8	A T 9 5	K J 7	A T 9 5	K Q 7 4	A T 9 5
J 6	K Q 7	J 6 5	K Q 7	J 5	K Q 7
A J 7	8 4 2	J 9 7 5 3	8 4 2	A J 5 3	8 4 2
78	**72**	**12**	**72**	**17**	**72**

1S	2NT(a)	1NT	2C	1NT	2C
3NT	P	2D	2NT(a)	2H	3H(c)
		P		(d)4H	P

(a) A balanced/semi balanced eleven to twelve, as over 1NT, remember?
(b) Sixteen to eighteen, balanced/semi balanced.
(c) The invitation is now made in hearts, not NT.
(d) On this hand as it turns out you may well go off in 4H; 3NT happens to have a better chance, but if the ♦KQ7 become the ♣KQ7 and the ♣842 become the ♦842, 4H is a better contract than 3NT.

HAND 73

On page 39 we met hand 73.

K 9 2	Q J 6	A K 9 7	Q J 6	K T 7	Q J 6
K J 4	A 9 6	7	A 9 6	K 8 4 3	A 9 6
A	Q 8 7 3	A T 6 5	Q 8 7 3	A J 5	Q 8 7 3
A J 9 7 5 3	K 8 2	A Q 9 5	K 8 2	A Q 5	K 8 2
35	**73**	**49**	**73**	**19**	**73**

1C	2NT(a)	1D	2NT(a)	1H	2NT(a)
(b)3NT	P	(c)3NT	P	(d)3NT	P

A T 9 7 2	Q J 6	A T 7 2	Q J 6	K T 9 2	Q J 6
K Q 7	A 9 6	K J 8 7	A 9 6	Q J 7	A 9 6
6	Q 8 7 3	A 6	Q 8 7 3	A J	Q 8 7 3
A J 5 3	K 8 2	J 9 5	K 8 2	Q J 5 3	K 8 2
84	**73**	**81**	**73**	**14**	**73**

1S	2NT(a)	1NT	2NT(a)	1NT	2NT(a)
(e)3C	4S	(f)P		(g)3NT	P
P				P	

(a) Eleven to twelve, balanced/semi balanced.
(b) Add 16 = 27–28, this is plenty, and the singleton is an A.
(c) Add 17 = 28–29; partner will surely have something in hearts, and I have no suit I want to play in.
(d) Add 17 = 28–29; not enough for a slam.
(e) Shows five spades at least and a club suit, therefore by implication some shortage; partner with three spades and twelve points bids game.
(f) I am minimum.
(g) I am better than minimum.

HAND 74

On page 39 we met hand 74.

A K	J 6 5 4 3	A K T	J 6 5 4 3	A T 9 7	J 6 5 4 3
7 3	A T 5	K J	A T 5	K Q 8 4	A T 5
A T 6 2	K 7	A T 6 5	K 7	A T	K 7
A J 9 7 5	K T 8	J 9 7 3	K T 8	A 9 3	K T 8
40	**74**	**22**	**74**	**25**	**74**

1C	1S	1D	1S	1H	1S
(a)2D	3NT(b)	1NT	3NT	3S	4S
P		P		P	

K T 9 7 2	J 6 5 4 3	A K T 2	J 6 5 4 3
K J 7 4 3	A T 5	K 8 7 4	A T 5
A J 5	K 7	A T	K 7
–	K T 8	9 7 5	K T 8
43	**74**	**55**	**74**

1S	4S	1NT	2C(c)
P		2H	2S(d)
		(e)4S	P

(a) A reverse bid is strong, remember.
(b) When your bridge is stronger and you read further you will find a better way to bid this.
(c) Stayman.
(d) Without my previous bid you would have thought this a weak take out.
(e) With a nine card trump suit known I am now worth sixteen.

HAND 75

On page 40 we met hand 75.

A K	Q J 8	K 9	Q J 8
7 3	A T 9 6 5 2	K J 7 4	A T 9 6 5 2
A T 6 2	K Q 9	A J T 6 5 2	K Q 9
A J 9 7 5	6	7	6
40	**75**	**80**	**75**

1C	1H	1D	1H
(a)1NT	4H(b)	(c)2H	4H
P		P	

9	QJ8	KT972	QJ8
KJ74	AT9652	–	AT9652
AT65	KQ9	AJT6	KQ9
AJ97	6	AQJ9	6
50	**75**	**47**	**75**

1H 4H
(d)P

1S 2H
(e)2S 4S(f)
P

AK	QJ8
KJ7	AT9652
J65	KQ9
J9753	6
12	**75**

1NT 4H(b)
P

(a) Balanced/semi balanced sixteen to eighteen points; remember, we met hand 40 on the previous page? Over partner's 1S response it made a reverse bid of 2D; however, ♥73 is nothing like such support as ♠AK, so with partner's strength in the one weak suit we think this a better rebid after the heart response.
(b) Partner has at least two hearts, giving the necessary eight card trump suit.
(c) Partner has at least four hearts, I have four, that makes eight, a trump suit.
(d) Note how in this deal and the previous one, because of the distributional nature of hand 75, what is important is winning top tricks; the ♠K9 is of no more use than the spade singleton, for all the high card point count; it is the switch to the ♣A that makes six likely, but it may not be easy for you to tell the difference yet, so be content with finding your solid games.
(e) I have at least five spades, and either don't care much for your heart bid or am not much more than minimum for my opening.
(f) 5 + 3 = 8, a viable trump suit.

HAND 76

On page 40 we met hand 76.

A 9	Q J 8 5
K Q 7	–
A T 2	K Q 8
Q J 9 7 3	K T 8 6 4 2
26	**76**

1C	1S(a)
(b)1NT	3C(c)
(d)3D	4C
(d)4S	6C
P	

K 7	Q J 8 5
K J 7	–
A J T 5	K Q 8
A J 9 5	K T 8 6 4 2
23	**76**

1D	2C
(b)2NT	3S(e)
3NT	4D(f)
6C	P

K T 9 7	Q J 8 5
K J 8 7 4 3	–
A J	K Q 8
7	K T 8 6 4 2
79	**76**

1H	2C
2H	2S(e)
3S	P(g)

A K T 2	Q J 8 5
K 8	–
J T 6 5	K Q 8
A Q J	K T 8 6 4 2
24	**76**

1S	2C(a)
(b)2NT	4S
(d)5C	6S
P	

K T 9 2	Q J 8 5
Q J 7	–
A J	K Q 8
Q J 5 3	K T 8 6 4 2
14	**76**

1NT	2C(h)
2S	4S
P	

K 9 7	Q J 8 5
J 8	–
A J 6 5	K Q 8
A J 9 5	K T 8 6 4 2
11	**76**

1NT	2C(h)
2D	4C(i)
5C	P

(a) Fit with partner can be shown later.
(b) Sixteen to eighteen points, balanced/semi balanced, not four spades.
(c) Forcing; the equivalent of at least an original raise to three.
(d) Cue bids showing the ace.
(e) My clubs are longer than my spades.

(f) Showing secondary support for partner's opening suit, and indicating not more than a singleton heart.
(g) On the high card and distributional values this would seem to warrant a raise to game, but the heart misfit changes the assessment.
(h) Stayman.
(i) I hold a two suited hand with long clubs which might be worth a game.

HAND 77

On page 42 we met hand 77.

A T 9 7	Q 8
K J 7 4	A
5	K Q 8 7 4
A J 5 3	K 8 6 4 2
48	**77**

1C	2D(a)
2H	3C
(b)3S	4H(b)
5C	P

A	Q 8
J 8 7 4	A
A J T 6 5	K Q 8 7 4
A Q J	K 8 6 4 2
44	**77**

1D	2C(c)
(d)2H	4NT(e)
(f)5S	5NT(g)
(h)6C	6D
P	

A K T 9	Q 8
K J 8 7 4	A
T	K Q 8 7 4
A 9 5	K 8 6 4 2
82	**77**

1H	2D
2H	3C
3NT	P

A T 9 7 2	Q 8
K Q 7	A
6	K Q 8 7 4
A J 5 3	K 8 6 4 2
84	**77**

1S	2D
2S	3C
5C	P

A T 7 2	Q 8
K J 8 7	A
A 6	K Q 8 7 4
J 9 5	K 8 6 4 2
81	**77**

1NT	3D
(i)3H	3NT(j)
P	

(a) I could bid 1D on six points; with the club fit I must tell partner how good we are.
(b) Cue bids showing the A.
(c) Not so urgent as in the last deal; I am already showing more than nine, the club suit is poor, and a jump would take us to the three level.
(d) The reverse bid to show strength; although here the hearts are horrible, you have good club support.
(e) **Blackwood**, remember; how many aces have you, partner?
(f) 5C=0 5D=1 5H=2 5S=3.
(g) Asking for K.
(h) 6C=0.
(i) There may be a four card major fit.
(j) But there isn't.

6 Strong Hands Opened with a Two Bid

As you already know, if you open the bidding at the one-level partner will usually pass with less than six points. This arrangement is satisfactory on most hands since the opener is limited to twenty-one points, and game is therefore very unlikely. However, consider hand 85:

A K Q 8 6 3	7
A K T 7 6 4	9 8 5 3 2
5	A 9 7 2
–	8 6 3
85	**86**

Sixteen points, only three more than the minimum needed to open a balanced hand, and two touching six card suits. If, following the rule of opening the higher of two equal touching suits you open 1S, what happens if partner holds hand 86?

There are just 4 points in it. That's right, partner will pass, and if the opponents don't intervene that will be it. So you will be playing in 1S with a game on in spades except against a few quite unlikely distributions, and a grand slam on in hearts!

Obviously, then, with this sort of hand, and even more so with stronger ones, we need a bid which tells partner to respond no matter how weak a hand is being held. In other words, we need **forcing bids**. For this purpose we reserve 2C, 2D, 2H, and 2S.

THE TWO CLUB OPENING

This is the strongest opening bid you can make in a **two club system**, such as the system called **Acol**. Acol is the most widely used system in this country; it is a very versatile and powerful system, and wherever we develop systematic usage we will lead you towards a sound version of it.

Unlike the other two-level bids, 2C is a conventional bid which has nothing necessarily to do with its own suit, clubs. In that respect it is just like Stayman. Consider hand 87; it cannot afford to have partner pass, but without even a five card suit to open, let alone a six card suit, and not having two suits and being able to open one of them, it has to be opened with a bid of 2C, *despite the singleton club*.

A K Q 5
K Q J 9
A K Q 7
3
87

Because it is conventional (some people use the word artificial) and not necessarily natural at all, it must be **alerted**, in the same way that we told you to alert the 2C Stayman response to 1NT.

The bid of 2C is game forcing except for one sequence only: e.g.

2C	2D	(The bid of 2D comes under responses below.)
2NT		which may be passed.

The **requirements** for a 2C opener are:

1 A hand with at least twenty-four points, *or*

2 An unbalanced hand with between twenty-one and twenty-three points which is likely to produce a game even if partner has nothing.

Identifying a Category 1 Hand

Since you can add up to at least forty this should be simple enough.

Identifying a Category 2 Hand

This is not so simple, because when you have an unbalanced hand with twenty-one to twenty-three points you do not necessarily have a 2C opener. However, at this stage of your bridge development it would be unreasonable to expect you to distinguish which hands in the range qualify for a 2C opening bid and which do not. As a guide, therefore, while you are accumulating the experience you need, we suggest that you open 2C if the hand has one suit with at least *some* positive bias and one suit with strong negative bias (*see* hands 91 and 93 below).

Here are some hands which qualify for a 2C bid:

	A K Q J 9 3	K Q J	A	A K 8 7 4	K Q 7
	K Q J	A J	K Q J 7	K Q J 4	A K Q 8
	A K Q	K J 3	A Q J 6 2	A K Q J	A Q J
	A	A K Q 7 3	A K J	–	A Q J
Score:	(29)	(24)	(25)	(23)	(28)
Hand:	**88**	**89**	**90**	**91**	**92**
Bias:	S++	H–	S––	S+	
	C––	C+	D+	C–––	

	8	5
	A K 9 7 5	K J T 2
	A Q 9	A K Q J
	A K Q 5	A K Q J
Score:	(22)	(24)
Hand:	**93**	**94**
Bias:	S– –	S– –
	H+	

Before we move on to the responses to 2C it is important that we mention strong two suited hands. Although many of these qualify for a 2C opening, in general they are better opened 2D, 2H, or 2S. This tends to make subsequent bidding much easier, especially if the opponents intervene. Hand 95 below, for example, which is similar but for its strength to hand 85 with which we began, is best opened 2S.

A K Q 8 6 3
A K Q 7 6 4
A
–
95

Responding to Two Clubs

When your partner opens 2C the first thing to remember is that you **must not pass**, no matter how bad your hand is. If you do, you may well find yourself looking for a new partner! So, what do you do when you are looking at a somewhat miserable collection? Well, in Acol we quite sensibly use the cheapest bid available, in order to conserve bidding space for partner to tell us more about this wonderful hand. In other words, we would bid 2D.

Like 2C, this is a **conventional** bid, the hand in question not necessarily having much in the way of diamonds, the suit ostensibly shown. For this reason it must be alerted by partner, just as you alert the opening 2C bid and 2C Stayman bid.

In answer to the opening bid of 2C, 2D is called a **negative response**. It puts a **top limit of seven points** on the hand, but says nothing about where the hand value lies between zero and seven. You have not said 'I have seven', you have said 'I have less than eight'. You may have none at all.

All other responses, **bids of 2H and above, are positive responses.**The requirements for each bid are as follows:

2H/2S A good four or five card suit and at least seven points. If you are minimum, that is seven exactly; you should have a good five card suit and an ace or two kings.
2NT A balanced hand with eight to ten points. The bid denies a five card major.
3C/3D A five card suit and at least eight points or an ace and a king. These bids consume more bidding space than 2H/2S and so need to be that much stronger.
3H/3S A solid six or seven card suit;
i.e. *A K Q J* 4 3 where there are *only six*;
or *A K Q* T 7 5 3 where there are *seven.*
This is a very rare occurrence and consequently many modern partnerships are not using these bids for this purpose. While you are learning, however, it is best to stick with the basics.
3NT A balanced hand with eleven or twelve points.
4C/4D As 3H/3S.

Now to see if you've got it right. What would you respond with the following hands if your partner opened 2C? Make a note of your answers on a spare piece of paper and then compare them with our recommended bids which you will find in the Answer section (page 156).

A J T 7 2	9 6 5	Q 6	9	K 3
Q J 6	5	Q 9 8 6 4 3 2	8 7 5	K 7 2
8 3	9 8 4	J 5	A K Q J 9 5	K 8 5 4 2
7 6 5	J T 9 7 5 4	J 6	6 4 2	Q 7 5
96	**97**	**98**	**99**	**100**

A J 8 5	K J 4	8 7
Q J 8 3	A 7 5 2	6 5
6	9 8 6 5	J 8 6 5
Q T 7 6	Q 8	A K 8 3 2
101	**102**	**103**

Further Bidding after a 2C Opening

After a Negative Response

When you open 2C, more often than not partner will respond with 2D. Quite naturally, you will feel disappointed each time this happens, but you can console yourself; after all, if you really did have your opening you are still likely to have a game on.

When you have a Minimum Balanced Hand (24–25 points)

You cannot be sure that game is on because partner might have absolutely nothing. When this happens, rebid 2NT, telling partner that this is the limit of the hand if partner has little or nothing. Other no-trump rebids show stronger balanced hands where you would expect to make the contract even if partner's hand proved to be worthless. Use the following ranges as guidelines, but don't be afraid to use your judgement when necessary:

with 26–28 points rebid 3NT
with 29–31 points rebid 4NT
with 32–34 points rebid 5NT

Partner is thus well placed to decide the level and denomination of the final contract. You may have the big hand, but once you have described it completely partner is in charge; for instance, if partner has a seven card heart suit and a void spade you are unlikely to find 4NT better than 5H; so *partner decides.*

When you have an Unbalanced Hand

You normally need to establish whether you have any kind of fit with partner before you can judge accurately just how much your hand is worth. It is important, therefore, to use the bidding space you have left economically; remember, you are already at the two level. *Do not* jump the bidding as many inexperienced players tend to do (possibly because they're afraid that partner has forgotten about their wonderful hand). The only time an immediate jump should be made is when you have a solid suit of at least six cards. This sets the trump suit and starts a slam investigation (*see* Chapter 9).

After a Positive Response

After a positive response you are in a very similar position to that which you find yourself in when you are responding to an opening one level bid. This is because partner has made the first natural bid in the auction (assuming the opponents have been silent throughout, as in this position they are likely to be). The principles are much the same, although no exact comparison can be made since the level of bidding and the point ranges involved are different.

This is not all there is to say, but the hands occur with comparative infrequency, so we will say no more about them now.

ACOL STRONG TWO OPENING BIDS 2D, 2H, 2S

These opening bids are generally reserved for hands which are too strong (usually in terms of playing strength) to risk a one level opening bid, but are either not strong enough or are too distributional to open with a bid of 2C. As with 2C, these opening bids are forcing, although now **for only one round**. There are two types of hand which should be opened in this way:

1 A single suited hand which contains at least eight playing tricks.

2 A two suited hand which is likely to produce game if a fit is found with partner in either suit.

Playing Tricks

Before we go any further it is important that we explain what we mean by playing tricks. When you hold a good (one or two suited) hand its potential is often not reflected by the high card points (HCP) held (remember hand 8 on page 14). This is because the HCP count does not take into account how the points, or the cards, are distributed in the hand. A better guide is usually obtained by estimating how many tricks you are likely to make if 'your' suit becomes trumps.

A K Q J 8 7 4
K Q J T 9 3
–
–
104

With spades as trumps you should expect to make twelve tricks with hand 104. The AKQJ of trumps would normally fell the outstanding lower cards in that suit, after which you can drive out the ♥A with one of your high hearts and establish the rest of the suit as winners. Of course, partner might have the ♥A, but remember you are only considering the playing strength of *your hand* , and to do that you must count on nothing from partner. Also note that in our example it is possible for an opponent to have five (or even all six) of the outstanding spades. Of course this is not likely, but how do you decide what is likely? Well, the easiest way is to assume that of the outstanding cards in the suit partner has just less than a fair share. Then imagine that the remaining cards are divided *unequally* between the opponents but in such a manner that *neither has three more than the other*. Let us consider a couple of examples.

First, take the spade suit above: 2H	**A K Q J 8 7 4**
Number of outstanding cards:	6
Average for each hand:	2
Assume partner has:	1
Assume opponents divide:	**3, 2** (not 4, 1 or 5, 0)
Tricks expected from suit:	**7**

This confirms our original assumption. In fact it tells us that we could replace the jack with a low card and still estimate seven tricks in the suit. Now consider this suit:

	A K Q 7 3
Number of outstanding cards:	8
Average for each hand:	2.66
Assume partner has:	2
Assume opponents divide:	**4, 2** (not 5, 1 or 6, 0)
Tricks expected from suit:	**4**

This time you must expect to lose a trick in the suit. After you have played the AKQ there is likely to be a card left outstanding. You must assume that it will be higher than your 7, and that it will be in an opponent's hand.

Values in your shorter suit(s) also require assessment. Obviously an A is worth a trick and an AK is worth two, while holdings such as Qx(x) or Jx(x) are worth nothing until we know partner's hand can help. But what are Kx or AQ worth? Well, assume that opponents will have to play on your short suits sometime during the play, which will give you a chance to finesse such holdings. Since a finesse is normally a fifty–fifty chance you should add on half a trick for each such. So Kx counts ½, AQ counts 1½, AQT counts 2, AQJ counts 2½, and so on.

This is yet another area where experience is invaluable, so you must not be surprised if you sometimes get things wrong – the most experienced players will still sometimes make mistakes. Only through regular play will you learn to judge the genuine potential of any given hand. It is important, however, that you work hard at it, for it is a vital area, especially for defensive bidding, to which we will be turning our attention shortly.

Now let us look at some examples of strong twos. Try to work out the initial playing strength of each hand, just as if you had just picked it up at the table, and then see if you agree with our estimate (given in the answer section). If you are within a trick in each case, fine. If not, read the last section again and have another go in a couple of days' time.

	A K Q 8 6 3	A	A K T 9 8
	A K T 7 6 4	K Q J T 9 7	K Q J T
	5	Q J T 8	A Q T
	–	A 3	5
Hand:	**105**	**106**	**107**
Open:	2S	2H	2S

	4	8 7
	A Q 8	J
	A K J 6 5 3 2	A K Q T 9
	K 7	A K Q J 5
Hand:	**108**	**109**
Open:	2D	2D

Responding to Acol Twos

Responding to an Acol two is very similar to responding to an opening 2C bid. The major difference this time is that partner has made a natural bid, so you have an extra option, that of supporting partner's suit.

The Negative Response 2NT

As before, when you have a poor hand you use a conventional bid to tell partner. This time it is 2NT, which must be **alerted**. Although you can have up to ten points for this bid it is only in extreme cases that you will find it necessary to give a negative or more than eight.

Positive Responses

All responses to an Acol two other than 2NT are positive to some degree or other, and can be summarised as follows:

A single raise of partner's suit: This shows support for the suit, usually xxx (three small) or Qx at least, with at least one ace in the hand. At least seven points are required for the bid. Do not make it if you have a good five card suit of your own in the hand (*see* page 81).
A double raise of partner's suit: This again shows support, although

usually better than xxx, but it denies an ace. Including distributional points the hand should contain between seven and eleven points.

The double raise is less encouraging than a single raise, for a simple and logical reason. If there is the chance of a slam you want to leave as much room as possible for the search. This is the principle of 'fast arrival' which will be met again.

A bid of a new suit: This will normally show a *good* five card suit, although it may be a four card suit if the bid is made at the two level. The requirements depend very much on what sort of fit you have with partner, if any. With good or reasonable support for partner (such as xxxx or Qxx) a suit headed by the AQ is definitely worth mentioning even if you have no other HCP. But why mention another suit when you have already found an excellent fit, you may wonder? Usually it is not because you want to suggest an alternative trump suit (although this is a possibility, for instance, if partner has opened 2D and you have a good major), but more because it may help partner in subsequent bidding. Without support for partner you should have at least nine points and your suit should, preferably, contain two of the top three honours.

3NT: This shows a balanced hand with ten to thirteen points which has no aces and a maximum of xxx in partner's suit.

Now let us look at a few examples.

Q 9 6 4	K 4 2	K J T 3	A 9
J 7 5 4	9 8 6	T 5	Q J 9 7 5
2	5 2	Q J 6 4	7 6 5
K 8 6 4	A Q 9 5 3	K 8 7	J 8 5
110	**111**	**112**	**113**

Say in each case what you would reply if partner opened with an Acol bid of: **1** 2D; **2** 2H; **3** 2S. Our opinion is available in the answer section.

Subsequent Bidding after a 2NT (Negative) Response

With a single suited hand opener will normally either rebid the suit or bid 3NT with eight or nine tricks that can be run. Such bids require no further action from responder, but if opener's rebid does not reach game responder should raise to game with any hand which is likely to take a trick in the play.

A rebid of a new suit below game by opener forces responder to bid again.

With a very weak hand responder should give preference at the lowest available level. With a good negative, that is, a hand likely to be as helpful to partner as a negative could be, responder can give preference at game level or if possible introduce a very good suit. For example, KQJxxx, which does not qualify the hand initially for a positive.

Subsequent Bidding after a Positive Response

The bidding after a positive response generally continues fairly naturally (that is, according to the principles we outlined for you earlier, over an opening of one of a suit) although after a single raise by responder a cue bidding sequence can be initiated by opener (*see* slam bidding page 109, Index, and Glossary). If you are going to use cue bids in this situation, until you are more experienced you should treat any bid of a new suit by opener after a simple raise as a cue bid. Blackwood is used when opener feels that a slam is on, unless two aces are missing (again *see* slam bidding, Index, and Glossary).

THE 2NT OPENING BID

On page 21 we gave you 13–21 as the range for an opening bid of one, with balanced hands dividing the range into three, 13–15, 16–18, 19–21, opening **1NT** with 13–15, rebidding NT at the lowest level with 16–18, and jump rebidding NT with 19–21. With 24+ points we have just told you to open with a bid of 2C.

This leaves a gap, the balanced hand of twenty-two, twenty-three which is opened with a bid of 2NT. In our earlier, low level, work we told you that you could open 1NT with a five card minor, but always to open a hand holding a five card major with one of that major. Now you will meet balanced or semi balanced hands possessing a five card major and twenty-two to twenty-three points which do not have enough playing tricks for **2H** or **2S**, so to indicate their strength they are best opened with a bid of **2NT**.

Responder's Action

Responder is in charge, just as in the 1NT opening. Opener has said it all in one go, except for fine detail, such as whether there is a four card major or not. It is not difficult to decide, as responder, whether there is enough for game, and often, if there is, what the game should be. As over 1NT, the Stayman convention can be used. Of course this time you are a level higher so 3C is the bid you use. Note that at your stage of play there is **no weak take out**; if you have very little, pass.

Q T 7 6 4 2	4 3
Q 8 5	K J T 7 5 4
7 6	K 4
T 6	J 7 3
114	**115**

1 If there is obviously a reasonable chance of a game in a major, bid it; you need at least a 6 card suit and 5 to 10 points (including distributional values). Hands 114 and 115 are examples, minimum and maximum.

8 7	Q 5
Q T 9	K 9 5
J T 6 3	K 8 4 2
J 9 8 4	Q T 7 2
116	**117**

2 Balanced hands with four to ten points and no four card major can do no more and no less than raise partner to 3NT. Hands 116 and 117 are examples, again minimum and maximum respectively.

J T 6 5	A J 9 6 5	J T 6 5
9 3	Q 9 5 4	4
Q J 9 6	7 6	J 9 6 2
J 8 4	J 8	K 5 4 2
118	**119**	**120**

3 With interest in the majors and enough for game, Stayman can be employed (*see*, for example, hands 118 to 120). Note that you use Stayman with hand 119 because partner might have four hearts. If 3D (denying a four card major), is partner's reply you can still bid 3S (forcing) to make sure you don't miss a five–three fit.

A K 8 7 6	9 8	8 7
5 3	A Q J 8 7 3	6 4
J T 5 3	A 6 3	K Q J 8 7 6
9 5	6 3	K 7 2
121	**122**	**123**

4 Other three level bids (3D, **3H** and **3S**) show exactly what they would do over 1NT – a game force with a five card suit. Look back to page 33 if you cannot remember what opener should do next. Note that with hand 122 you could bid 6H immediately but there is just a chance that 7H might be a good contract, and this is the best way to find out.

7 Pre-Emptive Opening Bids

The aim of the bidding we have discussed so far has been to exchange information with partner in order to reach the best contract possible. This is known as **constructive** bidding; you are constructing a sequence leading you to *your own* contract. However, you also need bids in your armoury which make it difficult for opponents and which give them the chance to go wrong. This is especially true when you know, or suspect, that they have the balance of the points. Since you are attempting to *disrupt the opponents*, such bids are called **destructive**, or defensive. Consider hands 124 and 125:

9	3
K Q J 8 7 6 5 4	–
T 8 7	K J 9 7 6 4 3 2
5	Q J T 5
124	**125**

These hands' HCP counts are respectively six and seven. By our basic standards they are both weak hands, hardly worth a response to an opening bid by partner, let alone an opening bid, if it weren't for their distribution. But just look at the playing strength of each hand. The partnership will surely finish in a contract based on your long suit, whichever of the two hands you hold. After all, you have an eight card trump suit even if partner is void, which is as much as you normally expect in any fit. You don't need bidding space, therefore, to search for fit, because in a sense you've already found it. There is one slight snag, though. What happens if partner isn't blessed with much in the way of HCP either? If you open ordinarily the opponents will outbid you, and your lovely hand will become practically worthless. Hence the development of pre-emptive bids.

When you make a pre-emptive bid it is normally because, although your partnership has established a fit, there is a likelihood of being outbid by the opponents, either because they have a suit outranking yours, or because you have insufficient HCP's. The aim of your bid now is not so much to arrive at a makeable contract (although this is desirable, and sometimes possible) as to deny the opponents bidding space, thus making it difficult for them to judge what to do on the hand. Obviously the earlier this can be done in the auction the better, and an opening bid is therefore the most effective pre-emption when the hand is suitable. Which brings us back to hands 124 and 125. If we open them **3H** and **4D** respectively, all the space up to those bids has been 'wasted' and denied to the opponents. Let us consider the problems you could cause.

A Q J 4 3	A T 4
K Q 7 5 2	9 7 3
Q	A Q T
K 3	A K 8 6
126	**127**

Suppose the poor devil sitting over you when you open **4D** on hand 125 holds hand 126. Its owner would have been expecting to open 1S . . . ! but what now? Partner may have four of either major, in which case there could be a game on; but then partner might not; it might be opponent on the left who holds six of the suit you choose, in which case trouble lies ahead if a bid is made. Any guess made might be right, but it could be horribly wrong.

On the other hand, in making these bids, you yourself run a risk. If instead of holding hand 126 when you make your **4D** bid opponent on your left holds hand 127, you have prevented nothing, because there is no marked place for that opponent to go. Instead, a nice fat penalty has been presented on a plate, and your grateful opponent, holding six tricks without help from partner, will double with alacrity. So we have to examine the optimum range for such bids, below which they are pointless, and above which the potential risks outweigh any gains.

A thorough excursion is more than you would want at the moment, so we shall show you a couple of examples to make the point, and then lay out for you the conclusions and guidelines drawn by those who have studied the problem very thoroughly.

EXAMPLE 1

Opponents can make 4S, you can make 3D. Scores NV and V are:

	NV	V
4S	420	620
5D–2	100	200
5DX–2	300	500

All these represent negative scores to you, positive scores to opponent. That means you are looking in each case for the lesser figure. It is easy to see that 5D makes a profit in every case except the one where you are vulnerable and opponents are not, when you give them 500 instead of their 420. So obviously the relative vulnerability has to be considered.

EXAMPLE 2

Opponents can make 4S still, but you can only make 2D. Scores now are:

	NV	V
4S	420	620
5DX–3	500	800

Now you only make a profit if you are NV and they are V, so the even more obvious point is that it matters how many you expect to go off.

An important point still to make is that if the opponents cannot make their game, which in going off gives you a positive score, any 'sacrifice' is **phantom**, converting not a loss into a smaller loss, but a gain into a loss. With the two hands we have given as examples you can see little likelihood of defensive tricks, which makes a large score for opponents more likely. The moment your hand contains defensive tricks, opponents' game becomes less certain.

SUMMARY

On what sort of hand should you open pre-emptively? It should:

1 Be a weak hand, because with a good hand you are not worried about the opponents intervening; you start the bidding at a lower level.
2 Contain few if any defensive tricks, for if it did contain defensive tricks you would be pleased to have the opponents playing the hand.
3 Be a hand which is dominated by the one suit, with you having no intention of playing in any other; the length of the suit is usually seven, and can be more. It can be six, but never less than six.
4 Have enough playing strength to stand a double from opponents.

Partner needs to be able to make judgements based on your bid, whether to raise you, and if so by how many, whether to pass, and so on. Partner should expect, and you should bear in mind that partner will expect,

that NV you expect to be 3 tricks light on your own hand;
and V you expect to be 2 tricks light.

It is now very easy for partner. Assuming that you have no outside defensive tricks, it is not difficult to add on tricks and see what can be afforded. Partner will know that you have few or no worthwhile cards outside your suit, and should only count sure tricks, such as A or AK. The arithmetic is simple.

Suppose you have opened **3H**:	NV 3H–3	V 3H–2
If partner can see two tricks:	+2	+2
This gives a total of:	3H–1	3H–0
And every raise subtracts another trick:	4H–2	4H–1
	5H–3	5H–2
		and so on.

A moment's reckoning shows what the profit limit is in the context of the deal.

One last look, then; beware the weak hand which appears to be pre-emptive at first glance but in fact is not. Compare hands **128** and **129** below with our original hands.

9	3	K J T 4	5 3
K Q J 8 7 6 5 4	–	Q J 9 8 5 3 2	J T 9 7 5 3 2
T 8 7	K J 9 7 6 4 3 2	–	A K
5	Q J T 5	T 4	T 3
124	**125**	**128**	**129**

Hand 128 may have a spade fit with partner, which a pre-empt would miss. There might even be a game on in spades and not in hearts. This allows us to formulate our first rule: **a pre-empt should be considered unsuitable as a supporting hand.** In this, hand 125 is an exception because the need to shut out opponents in both majors makes the pre-empt a lesser risk than that of missing a possible game in clubs.

Hand 129 has too much defence against any contract by opponents, while hand 128 has defence against a spade contract which partner could not expect. Pre-empting could therefore mislead partner into a phantom sacrifice. This takes us back to point 2 of our summary: **a pre-empt should contain little or no defensive capability.**

Pre-Empts in the Second Position

For all practical purposes pre-empts in the second position (when dealer, in 'first' position, has passed) are the same as the bids we have just discussed. There is still an opponent to come who may well hold the kind of hand you wish to pre-empt.

Pre-Empts in the Third Position

When you have a weak hand in this position a pre-emptive bid can be very effective indeed. Even when you hold a minimum opening hand now, it is quite likely that fourth player has a goodish hand, because neither your partner nor first opponent could open.

On the other hand, both opponents know that your partner is limited, whereas that wasn't the case before. On the one hand this makes it more desirable than ever to pre-empt, but on the other it warns a certain degree of caution, especially when vulnerable.

K 7
7 4
A K Q T 8 4
9 6 5
130

When NV, however, even a minimum opening hand with a good six card suit should be considered. For example, hand 130 above, which will not expect game to be on after partner's pass, may well talk opponents into a foolish contract if opened with a tactical bid of 3D.

The 3NT Opening

This is made on a solid seven or eight card minor suit and little else. Look at hand 131 below.

7
8 5 2
T 7
A K Q J 7 5 3
131

There are seven practically certain tricks in clubs, but if you get the lead in time there are, equally, seven tricks in NT. It is a pre-empt which offers partner a chance of game in either NT or the minor.

Partner is now in the driving seat. If there is a good chance of the game in NT partner passes. If, on the other hand, there is either a good chance of game in the minor, or partner can see disaster ahead on a bust, there is a need to know what your suit is.

First, the hand that wants to rescue into four of the minor. Partner bids 4C. If your suit is clubs you pass, while if it is diamonds you bid 4D and partner passes. However, if partner wishes to play in five of the minor the bid to use is 5C. Notc that your 3NT, and partner's 4C, 5C are all conventional bids.

Four Level Bids

These need hands containing a mixture of strength and weakness, especially in a major suit. Compare hands 125 and 132:

	3	K 8
	–	A Q J T 8 7 4 3
	K J 9 7 6 4 3 2	–
	Q J T 5	9 8 5
	125	**132**
Opening bid:	4D	4H

Note that 132 is almost good enough for an opening 2H bid, but the fact that it has so little defence makes the pre-empt the percentage bid.

Fourth in hand three and four level non-game bids are not strictly speaking pre-empts because both opponents have had the chance to bid, and they are not exactly frequent. They are used when you can see some competitive bidding ahead if you make an ordinary opening, and you don't want to be made to guess later on in such an auction.

8 Competitive Bidding

We have so far dealt with hands where we open the bidding and our opponents remain silent. It is a fact of life, however, that there are many deals where both sides have enough strength (not necessarily in points) to enter the auction. Most beginners regret this because it muddies the water, which is not always clear to start with.

Yet the contested auction is one of the most interesting areas of bridge, and will repay your attention to it many times over, both in terms of enjoyment and in terms of results. It is arguably the area of bidding where the greatest amount of judgement is required. We will give you good guidance about how and when to compete, but there will always be situations where only your own judgement can tell what is best. Remember our advice earlier about keeping a record of successful and unsuccessful forays, and adopt it here. The record will testify as to where sound judgement has been employed and where it has not.

1 There are two basic situations to consider:

1 When the opponents open the bidding and you intervene.

2 When you open the bidding and the opponents intervene.

In the second case they are presumably doing what we are about to teach you to do, i.e. how to intervene. It follows that if you understand 1 fairly well you have a better chance of thinking about 2 than if faced with it straight away. On the principle, therefore, of putting the horse before the cart we propose to deal thoroughly with 1, and leave the sometimes conventional methods which are used in 2 until your bridge is more confident.

When the opponents open the bidding at a low level you have four basic options available. You can:

pass
overcall (bid another suit or NT)
double
bid the opponents' suit.

YOU PASS

This tells partner that you have no wish to compete at this stage. The usual reason will be weakness, as in hand 134 below, but sometimes it will be because the distribution of strength in the hand is such that it is inadvisable to intervene. For example, if your right hand opponent opens 1S and you hold hand 133 below. Although you would have made the same opening bid yourself if there had been no bidding up to your turn, your best bet now is to keep quiet and hope the opponents get into trouble. You do not double yet, nor do you bid 2S.

A Q T 7 4	T 7 2
K J 6	9 5 4
Q 8 5	Q 9 7 3
6 2	J 9 5
133	**134**

Neither side is going to enjoy playing in spades, so you certainly don't transfer the problem from them to you, which bidding 2S would do. Nor do you want them to find a better spot to play in, so the last thing you do is to warn them (which a penalty double would do) until the bidding is so high that you are sure they have no escape. To double spades at a low level is futile, giving the opposition two options. They can either decide 1SX will make, and pass, when if they are right that makes your double look pretty silly. This is especially so if it is the information you've just given them which allows it to make, or they can find that better spot. However, if it was your partner who passed, suppose for the time being that the reason was lack of strength, because that is the more likely.

YOU OVERCALL

An overcall is a bid made in a new denomination after an opponent has opened. There are four ways in which you can overcall. You can:

	opponent's bid	your overcall
1 Make a **simple overcall** – you bid a new suit at the lowest permissible level. For example:	1H	2C
2 Make a **jump overcall** – you bid a new suit at a level one higher than is necessary. For example:	1D	2S
3 Make a **pre-emptive overcall** – you bid a new suit at a level two or more higher than necessary. For example:	1S	4C
4 Make a **no trump overcall**. For example:	1C	1NT

Simple Overcalls

When your opponents open the bidding they are initially at an advantage, in a similar way to a person playing the white pieces in a chess game. Because of this, when we intervene, we tend to have different objectives to those we have when we open. The main aims of a simple overcall are:

1 To make life difficult for the opponents.
2 To make sure that your side doesn't miss an opportunity to buy the contract should that prove possible, including making a sacrifice if that should seem advantageous.
3 To suggest a lead for partner in the event that you defend the hand.

The basic requirements for a simple overcall are a good five card suit (although a very good four card suit may be used at the one level) and between six and fifteen points. However, since a simple overcall is primarily a **destructive bid**, most important of all is to have sufficient *playing strength* for any bid that you decide to make. This is calculated in the same manner as when considering an opening two bid or a pre-emptive opening. The only difference is that when you value your finesse positions you must take into account the bidding so far. For example, an AQ holding in a suit that an opponent has bid should be upgraded if the bid was on your right, where the likely K will be trapped, and downgraded if the bid was on your left, where the likely K will beat your Q.

K Q J T 9 8	Q 8 7 6 4
4 3 2	K 7 6
4 3	J 6 5
4 2	9 8
135	**136**

Look at hands 135 and 136. With spades as trumps you will take five tricks with hand 135 no matter what, but with hand 136 one and a half tricks is all you can count on. As you can see, although both hands contain six points, hand 135 is far superior to hand 136 in terms of playing strength. This makes it a much more suitable hand for a spade overcall. To make a simple overcall you need a minimum of between three and seven playing tricks depending upon four factors:

Bidding space consumed.
Vulnerability.
The level of bidding required.
Your opponents' bidding.

Bidding Space Consumed

The more bidding space you consume the less strength you require. By devouring bidding space you deny to your opponents bids which they might usefully have used. It is the same idea that we met when we discussed pre-emptive openings, only on a smaller scale in that less space is usually denied, for example, if you bid 1S over 1C you stop them making any more suit bids at the one level.

Vulnerability

The more favourable the vulnerability the less strength you require. One thing you must always bear in mind when you overcall is that this will frequently become the final contract. If your partner has little or nothing you are unlikely to be able to fulfil your contract. Normally this should not worry you, because had you not intervened it is quite likely that your opponents would have made a contract of their own, doing just as well as a result, or even better. However, on the occasions **when you are doubled** you may find that this is not the case. Even two undertricks now could give your opponents far more than they were ever going to get without your intervention. This is especially so when they can't make a good game contract. In case you need convincing, look at the scoring details in Chapter 14 and see how expensive it can be. So, before you overcall, always check the vulnerability, count *your* playing tricks, assume partner will make no contribution, and then use the following guidelines:

Your vulnerability:	NV	NV	V	V	
Their vulnerability:	V	NV	V	NV	
Aim to be no more than:	4	3	2½	2	tricks light.

In hand 135, for example, with five certain playing tricks in spades (the solid suit can only lose once, to the ♠A, and there is not another trick in the hand) you can overcall at the one level no matter what the vulnerability, but if you had to overcall at the two level you should only do so when you are NV.

K Q J T 9 8
4 3 2
4 3
4 2
135

On occasion you will lose out because the cards are lying badly for you, but if your bid is well judged the opponents will have too little information to take punitive action most of the time. Count:

Tricks makeable:	**5**
Tricks contracted for when bidding one:	7
Deficit bidding one:	2
Tricks contracted for when bidding two:	8
Deficit bidding two:	3

The Level of Bid Required

The higher the level at which you have to overcall, the more playing tricks are required. If you overcall at the two or three level you are going to need more playing strength for the obvious reason that you have contracted to make more tricks. Further, you are more likely to be doubled for penalties at a higher level because your opponents require less to defeat you.

Your Opponents' Bidding

As discussed in Chapter 1, every call can help you to build up a better picture of the complete deal. When you are considering making an overcall you will only have one or two bids from the opponents to help you. However, quite often you will be able to deduce enough from their bidding to know whether it is safe to intervene or not. For example, you are West, holding hand 133 below (the hand on which you passed opponent's 1S on page 91):

A Q T 7 4 and the bidding starts:

N	E	S	W
1NT	P	2H	?

K J 6
Q 8 5
6 2
133

round the table to you.

From the bidding so far you can deduce:

	North:	13–15 points;	balanced hand; 2, 3, 4 hearts
	South:	0–10 points;	5+ hearts
And you	West:	12 points;	3 hearts
	Totals:	25–37 points;	10–12+ hearts
So	East (partner):	15–3 points;	3– hearts

Normally you would not consider intervening with 2S because your playing strength is not good enough. However, from what you have discovered about the opponents' hands (and consequently about your partner's too) there is much to be said for a 2S bid. Firstly, your partner is known to hold some points and could even have enough for your side to make game. Secondly, your heart honours are probably worth a bit more than four points now that suit has been bid on the right. Thirdly, and most importantly, is that *you are very unlikely to be doubled for penalties.* In order to understand why, you should look at the situation from North's point of view. South has promised nothing but five hearts and therefore could have no defence to a spade contract. In order to be confident of defeating 2S North must have six defensive tricks. However, even with some good spades and a maximum it is very unlikely that North could have enough sure tricks to defeat you and consequently will not be able to double you.

If the bidding started:

N	E	S	W
1H	P	2D	?

with the same hand, your deductions paint a far less rosy picture.

North:	13–21 points;	4+ hearts	
South:	8–15 points;		4+ diamonds
West (you):	12 points;	3 hearts;	3 diamonds
Total:	33–40 points;		
East (partner):	7– 0 points;		

Here a 2S bid would be unsound (a polite way of saying horrible). Your heart honours are badly placed, with the heart bid over you, your partner is known to have little or nothing, and you stand a good chance of being doubled by either opponent.

From the examples above you should be able to see why it is so important to bear in mind the opponents' bidding when considering any intervention. This is especially so when both opponents have bid without showing weakness, as in our second example. This is the most dangerous time to intervene.

Jump Overcalls

When the opponents open and you find yourself looking at a hand which has too much playing strength (7+ playing tricks) to make a simple overcall, one option available to you is a jump overcall. Unlike a simple overcall a jump overcall is primarily a constructive bid and requires at least the values you need to make an opening bid. Also, as it is quite likely that you will be playing the final contract in your suit, that suit should be a good one in terms of high cards held, and at least six cards in length. Below are some examples of hands which are too strong for a simple overcall after a one level suit opening bid from an opponent:

K Q J T 6 5 A Q 9 K 4 3 2 **137**	Fifteen points and seven playing tricks in spades. Over a 1C, 1D or 1H opening bid from an opponent, **bid 2S.**
A 7 A K T 4 2 A Q T 7 6 3 **138**	Seventeen points and seven playing tricks in clubs. Over a 1D, 1H or 1S opening bid from an opponent, bid 3C.
9 6 5 K Q J 9 7 6 5 A K 2 **139**	Thirteen points and eight playing tricks in diamonds. Here you bid 2D over 1C but, over 1H or 1S you bid 3D.
8 3 K Q J T 9 7 6 5 9 6 3 – **140**	Six points and seven playing tricks in hearts. Although you have sufficient playing strength for a jump overcall you do not now have the high card values required. However, as you will see in the next section, you have another option available.

Before we go any further it is worth making a couple of points. Firstly, like a simple overcall, a jump overcall is a non-forcing bid. Any hand containing nine or more playing tricks is, therefore, too strong for it (*see* page 103 for recommended action). Secondly, if both the opponents have bid and have used up a lot of bidding space, you may have to be content with making a simple overcall. For example, if the bidding went:

N	E	S	W
1H	P	2D	?

round the table to you as West, and you held hand 138 below, on which, over opponent's 1D, 1H, 1S you made the **jump** overcall of 3C, you do not jump now. You content yourself with the same 3C call. After all, partner is now likely to have less than three points, which means you will probably be struggling to make three, let alone four.

A 7
A K T
4 2
A Q T 7 6 3
138

Pre-Emptive Overcalls

A pre-emptive overcall is very similar to a pre-emptive opening bid in that it denies opponents bidding room. However, once opponents have opened you are more at risk, for opener's partner knows something about both the strength and the shape of opener's hand, and is better placed to make a punitive decision than when you open. However, that having been said, hand 140 below, which we saw on page 96, is entirely suitable for a 3H or 4H pre-emptive overcall, according to vulnerability.

8 3	3
K Q J T 9 7 6 5	–
9 6 3	K J 9 7 6 4 3 2
–	Q J T 5
140	**125**

The hands to be careful of are those like 125, where the trump suit is badly holed. Opponent sitting on your left with AQT8 of diamonds and little else will double in sleep now, where over your pre-emptive opening such action would have been dangerous.

The One No-Trump Overcall

As with an opening 1NT bid, and with NT rebids, we use a 1NT overcall to show a balanced hand and a limited point range. However, since one of the opponents has already opened the bidding we need to exercise a little caution. The following example demonstrates why.

	141 A Q 8 K J 6 5 7 2 T 9 5 3	
K 7 3 A Q 9 7 J 5 4 A 4 2 **142**	*N* *W* *E* *S*	9 5 4 T 8 3 2 9 8 6 3 Q 7 **143**
	J T 6 2 4 A K Q T K J 8 6 **144**	

Let us first consider the position if West has dealt. With fourteen points and a balanced hand the correct bid as opener is 1NT. This is likely to become the final contract. However, now consider the position if South has dealt. With fourteen points and 4, 1, 4, 4 shape South will open 1D. If west bids 1NT now, this is very unlikely to be the end of the story. In the first case, all North knew was that West had thirteen to fifteen, and the missing points could as well have been with East as with South. Now, however, North can deduce (with the aid of South's opening bid) that EW have insufficient values to make 1NT, and consequently can double for penalties. If NS defend well, West will make only two tricks in 1NT, because not only does North know enough to double, but also which suit to lead. Undoubled this is not good for EW (–250 NV; –500 V), but doubled it is disastrous (–900 NV, –1400 V).

In order to avoid this sort of result we recommend that you have **sixteen to eighteen points for an overcall of 1NT**. However, that alone is not sufficient.

A Q 6	K J 9 3
7 2	6 5
A K Q 4	8 6 3
Q 9 6 2	A K 8 5
145	**146**

South opens 1H. You as West hold hand 145 and partner holds hand 146. If you overcall 1NT (after all you have seventeen points and a balanced hand) your partner will correctly raise you to three (16/18 + 11 = 27/29, game should be on).

Which suit will North lead? Hearts of course, because South has bid the suit. The result of this should be that although you have enough tricks to make 3NT (four spade tricks, three or four diamond tricks, and three or four club tricks = 10/12 tricks), the opponents will take at least five tricks with their hearts **before you can obtain the lead.**

Clearly you need cards which will stop them doing this, called, not surprisingly, **stoppers**. That is, card combinations which prevent the cashing of the opponents' suit so that you can establish and cash your winners in time. Therefore, as well as having sixteen to eighteen points, you must have **at least one stopper** (*guard*) **in the opponent's suit before you can safely overcall 1NT.** Below are some examples of hands which could overcall 1NT after a 1S opening bid:

A J 9 5	K J 6	A K T	Q T 9 7	K 6	A Q J T 8
K 6 4	K 8 6 4	K Q 9	A K J 7	Q 8	K 9
K T 8	A J 5	Q J 9 2	J T	A K Q T 9	Q T 9
A J 3	A J 5	K T 3	A Q T	K 9 7 5	A 8 7
147	**148**	**149**	**150**	**151**	**152**

Hands 147 to 150 are clear cut, but hands 151 and 152 are not. Hand 151 is only semi balanced, and the stop in the opponent's suit is not that good. However, 1NT describes the overall strength of the hand much better than the alternative of a 2D overcall. Hand 152 has all the requirements of a 1NT overcall, yet there is a good case for passing, especially if the opponents are V. With such strength in your opponent's suit there is every chance that your best result will be obtained by defending against opponents' contract, possibly doubled. A bid of 1NT here may only be rescuing your opponents from disaster.

THE TAKE-OUT DOUBLE

So far in competitive bidding we have advised you when you should intervene with a **single suited** hand, and when you should overcall with 1NT. This is not the end of the story, there are other types of hand where intervention should be considered. The two main ones are:

Balanced hands which are too strong to overcall 1NT.

Hands with at least opening bid strength which have –ve bias in the opponents' suit, and no six card suit.

We shall deal with the latter type first and then show you how the former fits in with things. For example, your right-hand opponent opens 1H and you hold any of the following hands:

A K 9 7	K 8 7	J 9 5 3	A 8 6 4 3	Q J 8 7
7	9 8	Q	–	2
A T 6 5	A Q 9 2	A J 7 3 2	K 8 6 4	Q J T 3
A Q 9 5	K Q 8 7	A Q 6	A Q T 4	A K J 5
153	**154**	**155**	**156**	**157**

Each of the above hands has sufficient potential to justify an intervening call, given that partner is more likely to have a fit with you now that the opponents have bid your short suit. Our only problem is that we have used the simple overcall for quite different hands, and we certainly can't bid NT safely, or use the bids which show strength and/or a long suit. However, there are two calls which we haven't used yet. Indeed, one of them we have already warned you not to use; if you remember, it is a double of an opening bid in a suit when you hold that suit yourself.

So, we put our idle call and our need together and invent **the takeout double**. It says to partner, 'I have a hand strong enough to open, and it has support for any suit other than the one just bid by opener.' It has proved such a useful call that it is now used in many other situations where it is likely to be of more use than a penalty double. A guide line to start with is, **a double of an opponent's suit bid is for take-out** whenever:

partner has not bid;
the opponents have not bid game; and
it is made on the first round of bidding.

For example:

1	–	P	1H	X	X = double
2	1C	P	1S	X	
3	1S	P	3S	X	
4	3H	X			
5	2D	X			

Note that in example 2 the double would only promise support for the other two suits (hearts and diamonds). The exception to the rule is the double of an opponent's opening **1NT**, or **1NT response**. In each case the double regains its normal penalty meaning and should not be taken out unless you are very weak and have a 5/6 card suit to use in a rescue bid.

Now that we have solved the problem of how to intervene with the hands above, let us look at what action partner should take after we double. We shall assume for the time being that partner's right-hand opponent passes after the double, since this makes it easier to formulate guidelines. The particular situation we shall consider is this:

N	E	S	W
1H	X	P	?

It will help to think of West responding to an opening bid, except that partner (East) has effectively bid three suits at the same time, so you can choose which one to respond to, and you are usually forced to bid, except as in case 1 below.

K T
K Q T 8 7 6
9 5 4
8 5
158

1 Suppose you hold hand 158; the best final situation for you here is to have opponents try to play a contract in hearts. But if you **pass**, that is exactly what they will be doing, and doubled, to boot. To take this action you should have at least six cards (preferably good ones) in the opponents' suit and be reasonably sure that you cannot do better by playing in a contract of your own. You may sometimes have to choose this option because 'best' equals 'least bad'.

8 6 4
9 8 5 3
8 4 3
Q 8 4
159

2 Now look at hand 159. What on earth do you do if this is what you hold? Well, the one certain thing is that you must not pass, for that tells partner you have a hand like hand 158. 1HX will make, probably with overtricks, leaving the opponents frantically trying to compute the score, while your partner will simply be frantic. *You have to bid* unless right-hand opponent bids before you and lets you off the hook. Yes, we know how horrible your hand is, but look at the alternative . . . grit your teeth, bid 1S, and stand by to pass thereafter.

A 8 6 4 3	K Q
–	8 2
K 8 6 4	Q J T 5 3 2
A Q T 4	9 5 2
156	**160**

3 So what should you bid on hand 160 (after you've breathed a sigh of relief that it isn't hand 159, that is)? You might suppose that you should bid 2D, but a moment's thought should show you why that would be wrong. *You have to bid*, remember, and if you only bid 2D, which is the lowest bid you can make in diamonds, partner has no way of knowing whether you have a hand as wretched as 159 or one a little better. In fact, you are a lot better; you have eight HCP, and at least a nine card trump fit. Put it this way; what would you have responded if partner had opened 1D? For that, effectively, is the situation you must consider. You would bid 3D, so do that now. This is about the minimum for the jump, but remember, with this much *you must let partner know*. Because you are supporting partner you must bid to the limit. If partner holds hand 156, for example, you have a game on.

Q 9 8	K J 9 8
K Q 9 2	K Q 9 2
Q J 8 2	K 6 5
Q 6	5 2
161	**162**

With hand 161 you have a good guard in hearts, which makes NT the most attractive denomination of contract since your diamond suit would have to be bid to the five level for game, so you signal the fact with a bid of 2NT. The requirements are just as they have been before; eleven or twelve points, with a balanced/semi balanced hand, but this time guaranteeing a **sound heart guard**. This hand is an excellent example of the genre. However, if the diamonds and spades had been reversed, as in hand 162, it would have been tricky; spades might now be the best contract, and a better bid would probably be 3S. You will remember that we have met this comparison of major and minor suit contracts with NT before.

To Summarise

1 If you regard it as likely that the opponents' doubled contract will go off, and can see no better place for your partnership to go, then pass.
2 When you bid a suit it should be to the limit of the hand, so that partner can judge whether game is likely to be a good prospect or not. There is one exception, and that is dealt with under summary point 5 below.
3 Where you enjoy a five card suit or, failing that, a four card suit, priority should be given to showing it (except in the unusual situation posed by hands 158 and 161 above):
  a With 0–6 bid at the cheapest level.
  b With 7–9 bid at the two level even when the suit could be bid at the one level.
  c With 10–11 bid at the three level.
  d With 12+ treat as 5.
Distributional values should be included, since partner has guaranteed at least a semi-fit.
4 If the only four card suit you hold is the opponents' bid suit, tell partner via a NT bid at the appropriate level (unless you hold less than six points, when you must do as hand 167 had to do, which is to bid your first three card suit and pray). With thirteen points or more treat as for summary point 5 below.
5 When you know that the partnership has enough for game you should bid the opponents' suit to let partner know, so that the bidding is not allowed to die. It is a **game force**. It is not a natural bid, and should be alerted.
6 When you have very little except a six card suit bid by the opener, a pass is sometimes less damaging than a bid. Judgement is involved, and a consideration of the vulnerability. Do you want partner playing vulnerable and doubled in an unmakeable contract?

When Right-Hand Opponent Bids or Redoubles

Now the situation changes slightly, because partner will get another chance to bid. With a weak hand and no good suit you can pass and leave it to partner. Otherwise you should bid as before where possible and stretch slightly if you have to (it is now, after all, a competitive situation). Moreover, if you have managed a bid but opponents finally win the contract, partner will be in a better position to decide what to lead.

When Partner Makes a Take Out Double at a Higher Level

For example, with a take out double after a pre-empt at the three level, it is no longer possible to give such defined responses. It is difficult in this situation to give any definite guidelines, except that you should only bid NT with a sure stopper in the opponents' suit. Generally your choice will be whether to bid game or not, and here experience will improve your judgement. Note that partner should be stronger than when doubling at the one level.

Finally, *the hand which is too strong to overcall 1NT*. It is either so good that it wants to play in game somewhere, in which case it belongs in the next section (the cue bid overcall), or it is not. When it is not, double first, and bid NT over any response from partner. Partner will now know it all, will pass or raise as the case may be with a balanced/semi balanced hand, or will rebid a long suit at the appropriate level.

THE CUE BID OVERCALL

Occasionally a hand comes along where you are about to open with an Acol two when your right-hand opponent opens the bidding with one of a suit. This, of course, is very annoying, because a two level bid now would be non-forcing, regardless of whether it is a jump or not. Sometimes you could bid your own game outright, but that would sound pre-emptive, and partner holding enough to make the slam on would almost certainly pass.

Fortunately there is a way around the problem, and the nice thing is that in a way you make use of the very bid with which opponent annoyed you. You bid the opponent's suit at the next level. This is called a **cue bid of the opponent's suit**, as opposed to the cue bids we told you to use to show aces in earlier sequences. Like all cue bids it is forcing for one round. There is no danger of ambiguity, for after our frequent comments about the need for fit in the trump suit with partner, you will never want to play a trump contract of your own in a suit which the opponents can bid. We made a similar point at the beginning of the chapter.

So, if after opponent's opening bid you have a big hand on which you are interested in game, even when partner is weak, bid the opponent's suit at the next level. For example:

N	E	S	W
1D	2D!		

Such hands are rare, and we shall not elaborate upon them unduly, for you have enough on your plate already. They are usually single suited or two suited hands, and capable of at least nine playing tricks, like the examples given below.

A Q 8	A K Q T 7 4 3
A K Q J 3	A
K Q T 9 8	K Q
–	K Q 6
163	**164**

Right-hand opponent:	You:	Right-hand opponent:	You:
1C	2C!	1H	2H!
1S	2S!	1D	2D!
		1C	2C!

We can't leave the subject without explaining how your poor partner must cope. The only non-option is a pass. If the hand contains nothing worth showing, partner should bid 2NT, just like the negative to the opening bids of two of a suit. Otherwise partner must make the most informative bid on the hand.

When we discussed Stayman we told you to consider the frequency with which a particular bid occurred, and we abandoned a weak 2C take out in favour of a conventional asking bid. You will probably find more profitable ways to use the cue bid we have just been discussing when your bridge progresses further into the conventional field.

9 The Slam Situation

Slams are exciting, both to bid and to make. It is even exciting just to realise that there *might* be a slam on. Because of the enormous pleasure, not to mention the profit, from successful slamming due to the sizeable bonuses involved (*see* scoring page 151), we must encourage you to take the topic seriously, and, when the occasion arises, to have a go.

On the other hand, we need to strike a note of caution. Because slams are exciting it is easy to bid them on hope and excitement rather than on the requisite card holdings.

When you bid a slam and you do not make it, you lose not only the penalty points for your undertricks, but all those positive points you would have scored for the tricks you did make if you'd bid game only, and the *game bonus points* you would have scored as well. Consider these duplicate scores (*see* Chapter 14):

NV	4H+2	6H	
	120+300+60=+480	180+300+500= +980	Gain 500
	4H+1	6H–1	
	120+300+30=+450	–50	Loss 500
V	4H+2	6H	
	120+500+60=+680	180+500+750=+1,430	Gain 750
	4H+1	6H–1	
	120+500+30=+650	–100	Loss 750

Even undoubled you stand to lose as much as you can gain. If you bid all your fifty-fifty small slams throughout the year you will not quite break even, for some which go down will go more than one down. Nevertheless, many experienced players take this as their cut-off level.

We leave you to calculate the simple break even odds on grand slams, bearing in mind that when they fail you aren't just losing the game bonus points, but the *small slam bonus points* as well. With less experience and with the risk being so high, we suggest that whatever you find the true break even odds to be you don't bid grand slams unless they are a near certainty.

So, although we want to encourage you into looking for reasonable slams, and bidding them, we don't want you to become foolish adventurers. Reference to Chapter 5 will confirm our interest; in that chapter we bid to a slam in 23 sequences out of 162. It is significant that of those 23 slams only one was a grand slam. It is unusual, however, that none were in NT. No trump slams are bid not only on balanced hands, but quite frequently on unbalanced hands in order to avoid the risk of opponents getting an early ruff.

There are two fundamentals in the structure of a slam hand. Firstly, you need enough tricks, and secondly you cannot afford to have any weakness which allows opponents to take early tricks, for you have contracted for all but one trick, maybe every single one.

7 2	A K Q J 9 6 3	7 2
–	A K	9 8 6 2
A K Q J T 5 4	8	A K Q J T 5 4
9 8 6 2	7 5 4	–
166	**165**	**167**

Consider hands 165 and 166 with these two points in mind. There are only four spades and five diamonds missing, so playing in either suit against anything other than a club lead there are sixteen potential tricks. But if the opponents find a club lead you will lose three tricks before you get in. It follows, therefore, that before you commit yourself to a slam you should make sure this is not the sort of situation which faces you. Look at the difference if hand 165 is opposite hand 167; an almost identical hand superficially to 166, yet now the slam is on.

A 9 7	K 6 3
K 8 5 4	A 9 2
K 7 4	A 8 3 2
A 7 5	K 6 3
168	**169**

Now look at hands 168 and 169. Here you have every ace and king in the pack, yet there isn't even a game on unless you can find a 3, 3 break in either hearts or diamonds. The bidding (we hope) would go either:

1NT	3NT	*or*	1NT	2C
P			2D	3NT
			P	

according to which hand opened. So what becomes obvious is that:

1 We must establish that there is enough potential for a slam. This can only be done via the bidding; for example when partner has forced to game on the given information about your hand and you have more than you have shown.

2 We must have no more than one immediate loser; in other words, check that there are adequate controls. You can check this if necessary by means of cue bids, or by ace asking bids, or, indirectly, by a quantitative bid.

Let's look at some of the hands which we bid to slams in Chapter 5 in this way.

HAND 37 v 53

On page 45 we met the situation hand 37 v hand 53.

A	Q J 6
K 8	A T 5
A J T 6	K 9 7 3
A Q J 9 5 3	K T 4
37	**53**

1C	3NT(a)
(b)6C	P

Hand 37 has nineteen HCP, with S-- and H- if clubs or diamonds prove viable as a trump suit. (a) 13+ HCP. The failure to respond in hearts or spades shows less than four in either, not more than six in both. That leaves seven cards or more in clubs and diamonds. The failure to respond in diamonds shows fewer than five, and if there are as many as four there still have to be at least three clubs. A nine card suit at least, so besides S-- and H- add one for the ninth trump: 19+2+1+1=23, and partner has 13–15. Combined total 36–38. There must be lots of chances for at least twelve tricks. With first round **control** in three suits, and second round control in the fourth, there is no need to check with partner.

With an excellent chance of finding twelve makeable tricks, and with enough controls to stop the opponents stealing two quick tricks, (b) 6C.

BLACKWOOD

On page 58 we met **Blackwood** ace asking; hand 33 v hand 64.

A K T 9 7 2	Q J
K 4	A 9 2
A 5	K 9 8 7 4 3
A 9 7	K T
33	**64**

1S	2D(a)
(b)3S	4NT(c)
(d)5S	5NT(e)
(f)6H	7S(g)

(a) There are too many diamonds and too few clubs for a natural NT response.
(b) Partner has at least nine points, so there should be a game on somewhere.
(c) ♠QJ suddenly looks very good support after this bid. Partner has made a game force and I have rather more than I have shown. A slam must be worth investigating, so:
4NT: The Blackwood ace asking bid The bid is never natural except over a NT bid. It asks partner to declare the number of aces held by the following code:

5C = 0 or 4
5D = 1
5H = 2
5S = 3

after which 5NT asks for the number of kings in a similar pattern, except that now 6C is nought only and 6NT is four. There should be no danger of ambiguity in the 5C reply because of asker's holding and the bidding to date.
(d) 5C=0/4 5D=1 5H=2 **5S = 3**
(e) How many kings have you?
(f) 6C=0 6D=1 **6H = 2**

You now know that you hold all four aces and kings, and partner has at least six spades. There are, therefore (with your ♠QJ), six spade tricks at least, six outside tricks (♥AK, ♦AK, ♣AK), and you can reckon on either a club ruff in your hand or another trick from the diamond suit which can probably be established by ruffing; 13 tricks. Control: complete.
(g) 7S.

CUE BIDDING

On page 47 we met hand 46 v hand 54.

A	Q 8 4 3
4	A T
A J T 6 5 2	Q 7 4 3
A J 7 5 3	K T 7
46	**54**

1D	1S(a)
2C	3D(b)
(c)4C	4H(d)
(e)4S	5C(f)
(g)6D	P

(a) Although there is already a diamond fit, there may also be a spade fit, and if there is it will be more lucrative.
(b) The hand begins to look good. Partner almost certainly has five diamonds or NT would have been bid by now.

Now a trump suit has been established, **cue bidding** can commence. This is a system of bidding suits (other than the trump suit) **in ascending order**, in which you possess first round control, followed by suits in which you have second round control. Bidding is taken as far as necessary or as far as is safe, whichever arrives first.

(c) Shows the ♣A. On this occasion the ♠A is not shown immediately for fear partner sees 3S as secondary spade support (a).
(d) Shows the ♥A and definite interest in a slam.
(e) Shows the ♠A.
(f) Shows either ♣K or a singleton; second round control in either case after the ♣A shown in (c).

You will see that (f) is the crucial bid. The club suit can either be established or ruffed or both. There cannot now be two losers in the suit. The slam therefore becomes at least fifty per cent, for if partner didn't have sufficient trump strength two slam tries wouldn't have been made. This sort of judgement comes with experience, and is invaluable. There is, of course, the earlier truth we mentioned; your play has to be good enough to 'bring home the bacon.' Control: Complete.
(g) 6D (partner's 3D bid makes seven unlikely).

NO TRUMP SLAMS

You need to be able to count enough winners, and you cannot afford to be missing more than one ace or, at the worst, two kings. You can afford to have none missing in a grand slam. A tall order indeed. There are two basic situations to consider.

Situation 1

Two balanced hands opposite one another. Here it is simply a matter of counting points, because if you have the thirty-four points necessary for a small slam in this situation, or the thirty-eight points necessary for a grand slam, the controls look after themselves. You hold one of hands 170, 171, 172, 173 when partner opens 1NT.

Hand	
A K 8 A J T A 9 4 K J T 7 **170**	Count: 20 + 13–15 = 33–35 If partner is better than minimum there is a slam on. Bid 4NT to tell partner the good news (3NT wouldn't work, partner would always pass!). Partner with a minimum passes; with better than a minimum, bids six. Simple isn't it?
K Q J A T 9 A K 8 5 K J T **171**	Count: 21 + 13–15 = 34–36 There is enough for a small slam whatever partner holds, and not enough for a grand slam. Bid 6NT and again partner knows, this time passing in sleep, with no decision to make.
Q J 8 A K T A Q 9 3 A K J **172**	Count: 24 + 13–15 = 27–39 If partner is better than minimum there is a grand slam on, while if partner is minimum there is still a small slam. Bid 5NT to inform partner. With a minimum, partner bids six and with better than a minimum, bids seven.
A K 8 7 A Q J 3 A K Q K 4 **173**	Count: 26 + 13–15 = 39–40 Whatever partner holds there is a grand slam. The only point arising now is whether there would be any point in asking partner first whether there is a four card major in the hand. There is not! You would almost certainly find that there is no advantage; that there would be no losers to ruff, while if you choose to play in a suit and by some freak of fate one of the opposition has a void and you lose to a first round ruff . . .

The basic point to comprehend is that you play in a trump contract to gain an element of control which might not otherwise be there. Here you have all the controls you can ever need.

Note that in the situations described above *no ace asking takes place*, it is not necessary. There is an almost exact parallel when partner has opened 2NT. The differences are these:

Your point counts are less, because partner's are more.

Partner may have a five card major, so Stayman is relevant.

Situation 2

Quantitative bids create a problem, for occasionally you will pick up a hand facing a 1NT opener where you need to know specifically about aces, and now you can't ask with **4NT** Blackwood as you did in earlier situations.

A
K 7
K Q J T 8 5 4 2
K 3
174

Hand 174 is one such. There are obvious slam possibilities after partner has opened 1NT. If partner has:

three aces you want to be in 7NT;
two aces 6D;
one ace 5D;
no aces 4D.

There is a way to *ask* partner how many aces are held after a NT bid, and it is similar in its construction to Blackwood and the replies to that. The bid to use in this situation is **Gerber 4C**, and the replies are:

4D=0/4 aces
4H=1 ace
4S=2 aces
4NT=3 aces

partner	you
4D	Pass
4H	5D
4S	6D
4NT	7NT

Now, whatever partner has replied you have ended in the correct contract. Simple, isn't it.

Well, not quite. If partner bade 4D you would not now be in a game, so the question would arise as to whether you should convert to 4NT, which could be very risky against a spade lead and adverse spade holdings. Luckily, however, you don't have to worry, for partner won't do this. Can you work out why?

If necessary, Kings can be asked for over partner's reply by bidding 5C, and the replies are similar, only at the five level.

The following points should be noted with regard to slam bidding:

1 Do not use Gerber or Blackwood if partner can make a negative reply which takes you too high.
2 Neither Blackwood nor Gerber should be used with a hand which contains a void or a suit which might lose two quick tricks.
3 Do not ask for kings unless the partnership holds all four aces. Further, you cannot ask for kings without asking for aces first, even if you hold four aces yourself. The reason will become clear when we cover our next topic.
4 Only use Gerber directly over a NT opening bid, or it might be ambiguous.
5 There is no room for error in bidding or playing slams. Corollaries are that grand slams and NT slams should be rare.
6 In a suit slam it is safer to have nine trumps between you for extra control.
7 If after using Blackwood and finding you are missing two aces you want to play in 5NT you must not bid it; *partner will think you are asking for kings*. You must bid a new suit below 5NT, which instructs partner to make the desired 5NT bid. If you find yourself in this situation without such a bid you shouldn't have used Blackwood in the first place.

GRAND SLAM FORCE

One last goodie, the **grand slam force**. Partner opens 1S and you are looking at hand 175 below. You can see that partner may hold any number of point combinations involving clubs, and all of them are irrelevant. All that matters are the whereabouts of the ♠KQ. (Can you see where the D9 would go?)

A J T 7
A K Q J T 9
A K 9
–
175

A bid of 5NT tells partner you have a fit and that your only concern is with the quality of the suit itself, as in hand 175 above. It says to partner, if you hold two top honours, bid **seven**; otherwise, bid **six**.

The hand we have constructed would not be likely to arise, and, not surprisingly, any hand where the bid can be put to use is rare, but when the opportunity does occur it can be essential, as in the example above. Neither quantitative bidding, cue bidding, nor ace asking can procure the vital information.

This use of 5NT stops you asking directly for kings (*see* point 3 above). The bid can be used whenever you have established a fit and your only concern in considering a grand slam is with the quality of the trump suit.

10 Summary of the 'System'

Strength assessment: High card count A=4, K=3, Q=2, J=1

Requirements for an opening bid:
A At the one level:

In a suit 11 points and a six card suit.
12 points and a five card suit.
13 points.

Biddable suits: four to an honour or better.
Rebiddable suits: five to one of the three top honours or better.
Open: the longest suit;
or the 'higher' of two equal 'touching' suits;
or the major suit of two equal not touching suits;
or the suit below the singleton with a 4, 4, 4, 1 holding.
Exceptions where you open with a heart:
4, 4 in spades and hearts;
4, 4, 4, 1 singleton club.
1NT 13–15 and a balanced hand (4, 3, 3, 3; 4, 4, 3, 2; 5, 3, 3, 2)

B At the two level and above:

2C	A game going hand or 24–25 balanced.
2D, 2H, 2S	Eight or more playing tricks, *or* a two suited hand likely to produce game with a fit.
2NT	22–23 balanced.
3/4C, D, H, S	6+ playing tricks based on the rule of 3 and 2; little defence.
3NT	Solid minor suit, little outside.

Responding to partner's one of a suit opening:
With four card support 6–9 raise once;
10–12 raise twice;
13–15 raise to game if a major.
(The point counts include any distributional values.)

Other responses:

limited		unlimited	
1NT	6–9	new suit at the one level	6+
2NT	11–12 balanced	new suit at the two level	9+
3NT	13–15 balanced	jump in new suit (forces to game)	16+

Responding to partner's 1NT opening:

balanced hand		unbalanced hand	
0–10	pass	0–10	bid a (2D, 2H, 2S) weak take out or pass
11–12	2NT or Stayman 2C	13+	bid 3C, 3D, 3H, 3S five card suit, game forcing
13–19	poor 3NT or Stayman		
19+	slam situation		

Responses to 2C:
2D negative; 0–7.
All other bids are positive and show 8+.
When opener rebids 2NT over 2D or when **responding to a 2NT opening,**
3C is Stayman, game forcing;
3D, 3H, 3S show a five card suit, game forcing.

Responses to 2D, 2H, 2S:

2NT	negative	0 to a very poor 10
new suit	positive	7+
raise once	positive	an ace + support
raise twice	positive	no ace but support

Slam methods:
Cue bids to check controls once a suit fit is found.
4NT Blackwood ace asking.
4C Gerber ace asking directly over a 1/2NT opening.
4NT, 5NT bids over opening 1NT, 2NT; quantitative, invitational to 6, 7.
5NT grand slam force.

Defensive bidding

Simple overcalls:
A good five card suit; six to fifteen points. Playing strength is the main guide.

Jump overcalls:
Too strong for a simple overcall but fits no other category.
Opening bid strength, and at least a six card suit.

Pre-emptive overcalls:
Similar to pre-emptive opening bids.
The one no-trump overcall:
A balanced hand of sixteen to eighteen with opponents' suit stopped.
The take out double is made on:
A balanced hand which is too strong to overcall 1NT, *or* a hand with at least opening strength, –ve bias in opponents' suit, and no six card suit.
Responder's action to the take out double:
Make any suit bid to the limit of the hand.
Bid NT at appropriate level if you hold stops in the opponents' suit.
Bid the opponents' suit if there is enough for game.
Pass with length and strength in the opponents' suit.

Cue bid:
Shows a strong one or two suited hand.

11 Play

The play is a battle, between declarer and the defenders, and it may well add interest to the game if you learn to see it as such. It is a kind of fencing match, with thrust, and parry, and feint.

In this chapter we will consider the play from the declarer's point of view, but even so you should pick up defensive tips along the way. Learning to play hands well as declarer must eventually benefit your ability to defend.

To become a good bridge player you need to be able to play the cards well, otherwise you will never realise the full potential of your hands. Since there is nothing more demoralising than going down in contract after contract we have recommended point values which offer you some leeway as declarer while you are learning. The point is that, although the primary aim of our bidding is to arrive in the best contract available, the description 'best' has to relate not only to the contracts possible on the cards we are dealt, but more realistically to those contracts we are capable of making.

The first thing you must master is the initial impulse. When the dummy is displayed after the opening lead it is important to pause and consider, regardless of the denomination and level of the contract. It is the last time you will see the total assets of your side. You need to assess the possible, and then the most probable implications of the lead. You need to assess the number of safe tricks, the number of sure losers, and what these figures tell you about the likelihood of success in your contract. If you have enough safe looking tricks you will aim for safe plays, in order not to lose any unnecessarily, while if you have a shortage of sure tricks you must assess the merits of any plays available to manufacture extra ones. In this way you **develop a line of play**.

Although it is highly unlikely that you will ever meet the same hand twice, patterns recur, and there are therefore basic techniques which you will find useful time and time again. Two of the most important ones are:

establishing winners;
finessing.

ESTABLISHING WINNERS

It is important that you understand this process thoroughly. There are two essential methods.

Establishment by Force

Establishment by force is driving out high cards held by the opponents in order to leave you with masters. For example,

(i) K J x Q x x (=K x J *v* x Q x= K Q J *v* x x x)
With this combination two tricks can be established by using one of the honours to force out the ace.
(ii) Q J x T x x (=Q J T *v* x x x)
Only one trick can be established in example (ii) as both the ace and the king need to be forced out.
(iii) J T x x 9 8 x (=x x T J *v* 8 9 x = 8 9 T J *v* x x x)
Although you are missing the ace, the king, and the queen, a trick can still be established because you have four cards in one hand and a combined sequence headed by the jack.

Before we move on, a few words of warning. Firstly, when establishing winners in short suits, that is, in suits where your combined holding is six or less and the opponents' is seven or more, make sure that you don't end up establishing vital winners for the opponents, especially in NT. In example (ii) above, for instance, assuming a NT contract for simplicity, you will probably find that the opponents are only too willing to give you your trick in order to establish one or two of their small cards in the process.

Secondly, only when winners have been established can they be counted as such. This is an important point to remember, especially in NT, when sometimes you do not have time to establish all your winners because the opponents have established too many of their own first. For example,

♠3

West		East
K 7	*N*	Q 9
A Q J 5		K 8 4
A Q T 6	*W* *E*	J 9 3 2
K Q J		T 7 6 5

Contract, 3NT by West; lead, ♠3 (fourth highest?). South wins with the ♠A and returns a spade. This leaves you with one trick and no spades whatsoever, while the opponents have one trick, five spades, and the ♣A between them. Since the spades will probably break 3, 2, when they get in with the ♣A you can see yourself losing three more spade tricks:

1♠ + 1♣ + 3♠ = 5 tricks, one off.

The defence has established enough winners to take you off the moment you lose the lead, which you will do the moment a club is led. Ergo, you dare not lead a club to establish sure tricks for later, for by then it will be too late. It is neck or nothing; you have one trick and need eight more, which must come from four hearts and four diamonds.

Your only realistic chance of making the contract is to finesse in diamonds even though you may go two down as result.

Play on clubs: 1 down.

Finesse the diamond: make or 2 down.

Establishment by Exhaustion

Establishment by exhaustion means exhausting the opponents' holding in a suit where yours is greater than theirs. For example,

(i) A Q x x K x x

With this combination you are certain of three tricks, but when the outstanding cards in the suit are divided 3–3, a fourth will be established once you have played the AKQ (not necessarily in that order). The chances of success in this situation are not as great as you might think, because when there are six cards missing they divide:

6,0 1% of the time;
5,1 15% of the time;
4,2 48% of the time;
3,3 36% of the time.

That is, they break worse than 3, 3 64% of the time, with 4, 2 the most likely split. It is usually best, therefore, not to tackle this sort of combination early in the play because it is more likely to establish a trick for the opponents. When possible, wait until near the end of the play, in the hope that an opponent with length in the suit may make the mistake of discarding from it.

This timetable-building is precisely what we had in mind when we spoke earlier about developing a line of play.

(ii) K Q x A x x x x

Again you start with three obvious tricks but this time there is a good possibility that you will establish two extra tricks when you cash the AKQ. This time, with only five cards missing, the likely divisions are:

5, 0 4% of the time;
4, 1 28% of the time;
3, 2 68% of the time.

This gives odds of practically two to one in favour of a 3, 2 split. Without listing all the odds in this fashion, we offer this simple rule;

When an **odd** number of cards is missing **they are likely to break well.**

When an **even** number is missing **they are likely to break badly.**

Note: When you play on a suit like this it is normally correct to cash the honours on the short side first to ensure that you do not get cut off from any winners you establish.

(iii) x A K x x x x

Here we have a less promising situation initially, in that we only have two definite tricks. In NT there is no way in which we will be able to establish the suit without losing at least one trick along the way, for with six cards missing the best you can hope for is a 3, 3 break. However, it is a suit worth persevering with if you have the entries, for you could finish with four or five tricks for the loss of only one or two.

In a suit contract you may be able to do better, for you no longer need lose any tricks in the suit, because you will be able to ruff after the first round of the suit has been played. This will depend on other things as well, of course, such as the number of trumps you have, and the number of entries (as before), but you should grasp the idea.

FINESSING

A finesse is a manoeuvre with the aim of taking a trick with a card (usually an honour) which can be beaten by an outstanding card held by the opponents.

There is usually an element of risk involved because you are unable to see the opponents' cards, so you cannot be sure who has what. When helpful information gained from the bidding or from the early play enables one to take a particular finesse knowing that it should succeed, that finesse is known as a **marked** finesse. Obviously, the more of these you can take the better.

So let us look at the various types of finesse that exist. In each example the first card you lead is written in bold.

The Simple Finesse

	West	East
(i)	K x	x x **x**

This could not be simpler. If South plays the ace you play small and if not you play the king. With nothing to guide you, assume your chance of success to be 50%.

(ii)	A Q	x x **x**

This is very similar; you play the queen unless South plays the king. Again your basic chance of success is 50%. You will make your ace later of course whether the queen wins or not.

(iii)	Q x x	A x **x**

This is in essence the same as (i), where the trick may be lost to either defender. Don't start by leading the queen, though; this will reduce your chance of a trick with it to zero, for now either opponent can cover it.

Note: In this case no outside entry is required to the East hand to take the finesse because you can use the ace in the suit as such. However, if you do that and the finesse loses you lose control of the suit, for you no longer have a master in the suit. This might be important, especially in NT.

The Repeated Finesse

	West	East
(iv)	A Q J	x x **x**

This is an extension of the position we have just seen in (ii) above. Once the finesse is successful on the first round, if you can return to the East hand you can repeat the procedure. If South has the king you then end up with three tricks, while if North holds it you only make two.

Note: Don't be lulled into a false sense of security if the first round finesse succeeds. A crafty North may well cause you to waste an entry to the East hand by keeping the king for when you try the second finesse. This is an example of what is called **a hold up play**; you will meet others.

(v)	K J T	x x **x**

We can establish one trick in this suit by force, just as we could have established two in the previous example, but if the queen is with South we make two tricks by finessing, provided of course that East has sufficient entries. Play the jack, or ten, on the first round (unless the queen appears, when you will cover with the K). If North then wins with the ace, regain the lead in East's hand and repeat the process. Similarly if the jack, or ten, holds the first trick.

(vi) Q T 9 x x **x**
This position is the same as (v) except that all you can hope to establish is one trick. This time you need South to have the jack.

The Double Finesse

This is a finesse taken against two cards simultaneously.

West East
(vii) A J T x x **x** K Q missing
On the first round, play the jack (or ten) unless South plays an honour. Assuming that this loses, which is more likely than not, you have this position left: A T x **x** with one honour missing. Regaining the lead in the East hand, you finesse again. Unless North started with both the missing honours you will make two tricks. This is a 75% chance.
(viii) A Q T x x **x** K J missing
Here you can give yourself the chance of three tricks by finessing first the ten and then the queen. If South has both the king and the jack you will be successful. This is only a 25% chance, but as it does not affect your chances of making two tricks in the suit it is worth trying. Finessing the queen on the first round cannot achieve three tricks (unless North has the singleton jack), but is the better play if two tricks are your priority.
(ix) A K T x x **x** Q J missing
Again you can make three tricks if South holds the missing honours. Play the ten on the first round if South plays low. If South plays an honour, cover, and then repeat the procedure if possible. Only a 25% chance again, but still much better than trying to drop the queen and jack by playing the ace and king on the first two rounds.

The Two-Way Finesse

West East
(xi) A J x **x** K T x **x**
With our previous examples there was only one way to take each finesse. If you had known where the honour(s) were against which you were finessing it would have made no difference. They were either on the right side or the wrong side, and that was that. Now, however, if you knew on which side the queen lay you could guarantee to finesse it successfully, whichever side that was. The finesse would be marked. As it is, you will probably guess. The trouble is that when it comes to guessing the experts seem to guess right far more often than we do, and the suspicion grows that this may not be pure coincidence.

It may have something to do with listening to the bidding, thinking about the leads that have been made, and counting the points which have appeared from each opponent during the play so far. What do you think?

If in fact there is no way to mark the finesse there is still a priority we can apply to our choice. We can decide which is the safest direction to take it in. By this we mean taking it in such a direction that, if it fails, the opponent who is least capable of a damaging play is left on lead.

Note: Here the finesse is more likely to succeed than an attempt to drop the queen by playing out the A K, but with a nine card combination the odds favour the drop. (Some people remember this by saying 'eight ever, nine never'; heaven alone knows why.)

(xii) Q T **x** K 9 **x** A J missing

Here, although you must certainly lose to the ace, if you finesse successfully against the jack you can still come to two tricks.

Note: Always lead small if you can; from time to time you will find your problem solved by the appearance of a singleton high card.

Entries

We have been talking about entries all through this section on finesse, and it should have dawned on you that they are of some importance. They are in fact vital, being the crux on which we achieve communication. The communication problem is often the main stumbling block for the learner, and the last to be overcome, if ever.

Entries are precious, and should be conserved for the right moment, or even created if there is a natural dearth. The following example may help to show you why.

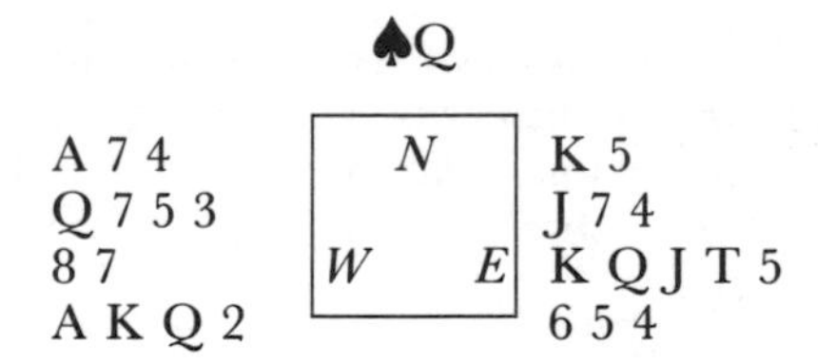

Contract: 3NT by West. Lead ♠Q.

Suppose you aren't one of our readers, and you say, 'put the K on, partner' almost before dummy is down. Now you stop and take a belated look around, and tell partner to play the ♦K. South duly plays the 4, you play the 7, and North plays the 2. 'Play the queen' you say, and the 3 appears from South, you play the 8, and North wins with the ace. With the position now:

A 7	5
Q 7 5 3	J 7 4
–	J T 5
A K Q 2	6 5 4

North plays another spade! You are going to end up with tricks from the ♠A, ♠K, ♦K, ♣A, ♣K, ♣Q and a trick from the ♣2 if the clubs break before you lose out to ♥A, ♥K, and two or more spades, which with the ♦A makes one or more down, with three perfectly good tricks sitting wasted in dummy.

Take with the ♠A in hand (and don't duck the first round, or the ♠K will be bared and you will have to play it and be back with the situation we've just seen). Now when you have forced out the ♦A the ♠K is waiting as an entry for the JT5, which the unhappy non-reader above failed to use.

Small trumps can be used as entries in certain situations. For example:

♠5

W	N / W E	E
A K Q J		8 7 6 4
8 7 6 4 3		–
–		A K Q J 7 6
A K 4 2		7 6 5

Contract: 4S by West. Lead ♠5.

Here a heart may be ruffed to gain entry to dummy's diamonds for at least two heart and two club discards, and on the hand it is the only way to get there. With such a long diamond suit it would be advisable to draw two rounds of trumps first to guard against a damaging amount of ruffing by the opponents.

Playing from the Short Hand First

This is done to maintain communication and is something that beginners often have great difficulty with. The reasons are various. They certainly tend to 'forget' dummy, treating it as some kind of poor relation. Sometimes they forget that you have to lead from the hand which won the last trick, and they often don't plan the hand early enough (if they plan at all).

Now look at these examples, where the high cards are played from the shorter holdings first:

Kx AQJx = Kx*v*xAQJ = xx*v*KAQJ = xx*v*AKQJ
and here A=K=Q=J

It is in terms of trick winning potential that they are equal, for opponents have no cards with which to beat any of them. So play the K first and then cross with the small remaining card to the AQJ. If you play the A first, K QJx !

QJx AKxx Play the QJ first, throwing the two small cards from East's hand on them, then use West's third card to cross to the AK.

AJT9 KQ Play the K, and then overtake the Q with the A (A=K=Q=J=T=9).

When you fail to play these and similar holdings in the way we've shown you, you have to use up other entries which you should probably have been saving, and frequently this leads to a total breakdown of communication between the two hands, with a consequent failure to make what ought to have been a stone cold contract.

With the examples above as a guide, see if you can make this one:

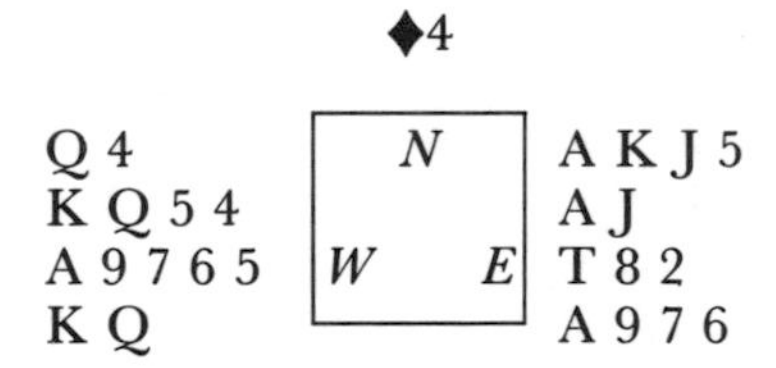

Contract: 6NT by West. Lead ♦4.

You will find a recommended line of play in the answer appendix.

We shall now turn our attention to the play of complete hands.

NO TRUMP CONTRACTS

In NT contracts you plan the play initially by considering the number of certain winners you have between the two hands, in other words, tricks which can be cashed. Occasionally there are enough to ensure the contract, so all you have to do is obtain the lead and cash them in some sensible order. However, you all too often find that there are not. You must then consider each suit in turn for tricks which can be developed by the techniques we have shown you. This should give you an indication of which suits to attack. Now for some example hands.

Do you recognise the table below? If you remember back on page 12 we left you (as South) to decide whether or not it was best to win the opening lead. Before we come back to that particular problem let us consider the hand as whole and form a general plan.

	North	
	K T 8 2 A J 2 8 4 Q J 8 3	
West x x x x x x x x x x x x x	*N* *W* *E* *S*	**East** Q x x K Q x x K x x A x x
	A J 3 8 5 3 A Q J 7 2 K 4	

Bidding:	N	E	S	W
		1NT	2D	P
	2NT	P	3NT	P
	P	P		

Lead ♥K

Plan:

Winners:	Spades	2
	Hearts	1
	Diamonds	1
	Clubs	0
	Total	4

Things don't look too promising, but let's take a closer look at each suit.

Spades If you get the two-way finesse right and a 3, 3 break you could end up with **four** tricks without loss. 4

Hearts Not a great deal we can do here, although if we duck the lead (let West have the first trick) we might get a heart continuation which would give us **two** tricks. 2

Diamonds With repeated finesses against the king and a 3, 3 break

you might end up with **five** tricks. However, three or four are more likely. 5
Clubs Two tricks can certainly be established, and there is a remote chance of a **third** if the ten and nine fall on the first three rounds. 3
Total possible winners: 4+2+5+3 = 14!

Surprisingly enough, we are going to tell you not to worry too much about the (14–4) total trick difference; the 14 tells us we have good chances. What are important are the individual suit differences, S(4–2); H(2–1); D(5–1); C(3–0). We look for the source of most potential, and see D, C, S, H in order. Now, if you remember, we know where all the high cards lie. What we're not certain of is the precise distribution, although we do know that East is balanced. We make a note that it will be irresponsible to take any finesses into East's hand.

Firstly, you should ask, should we take the ♥K? Well, if we do we certainly won't get the continuation which will give us two heart tricks, so let's suppose we duck it. What can East do then? After a look at dummy, the answer is probably lead a club. North has the QJ8, with only the T9 missing, so that would be good, giving you an extra entry to finesse the spades in due course as well as the diamonds.

It is therefore possible to duck the ♥K, win the likely club continuation with either the 8 or the J, and then start on the diamonds with finesse one. Return to the ♠K, and take diamond finesse two. Cash ♦A, and see if the suit breaks 3, 3. If it does, cash two more diamonds, and if it doesn't, play a diamond to establish the fifth one.

If they broke, 1S+5D+1C, the ♥A to cash, and the spade finesse to come makes the contract safe with an overtrick. If they didn't you have 1S+3D+1C with either W or E on lead according to who won the diamond. There is still the ♥A to win, the spade finesse for another two tricks, and the fifth diamond to cash; nine tricks.

Let us look at a more normal situation where you have learnt nothing about the opponent's hands from the bidding and as a consequence have to make more assumptions about the possible lie of the cards.

South leads ♠5 (fourth highest?)

(W)	(E)
Q 6	A 9 7
K 6 4	A 3
K J 9 4	A T 7 5
A J 7 5	K T 5 3

Plan:

Winners:		
	Spades	1
	Hearts	2
	Diamonds	2
	Clubs	2
	Total	7

(two tricks short)

Bidding:	N	E	S	W
	–	–	1NT	P
	3NT	P	P	P

♠7 to the ♠Q will gain a trick if West has the ♠K. +1
Nothing extra can be won in hearts. 0
A two-way finesse offers the possibility of two more diamond tricks. +2
A two-way finesse offers the possibility of two more club tricks. +2
Danger: If the spades are breaking 5, 3 or 6, 2 and ♠K is with North.
The Play: Put up the ♠Q, because South may well have led from the king. If it holds, play on diamonds (better than clubs) to establish a ninth trick while you still have control of the spade suit. If the ♠Q is covered by the king, duck, and duck a spade continuation in an attempt to cut the opponents' communications. When you win with the ♠A, take the finesse in diamonds *through South* (the danger hand). If it wins, you are home. If it loses and the spades are 5, 3 or 6, 2, you are safe because North doesn't have a spade left to lead and you can establish an extra club trick in the same manner. If the spades are 4, 4, however, your contract now depends on the club guess.

(W)	(E)					
7 6 5	A Q 3	Bidding:	N	E	S	W
A K 6 5	J 4 3		–	–	–	1NT
K 8	A J 2		P	3NT	P	P
A 6 5 4	K Q 7 3		P			

North lead ♣2

Plan:
Winners:

Spades	1
Hearts	2
Diamonds	2
Clubs	3
Total	8 (one trick short)

Just one trick short can't be bad, but that final winner can be the hardest to come by, so we had better take a closer look.
Spades A simple finesse could give us an extra trick. +1 2
Hearts Similarly here where we can lead a low card towards dummy's jack and hope that North has the queen. Also there could be a 3, 3 break for a trick. +1 3
Diamonds Again we have a finesse position which might provide the extra winner. +1 3

Clubs Normally we would expect this suit to break 3, 2 (a favourable odd number) to provide us with four tricks. However, the opening lead (assuming the opponents are playing fourth highest) tells us that we should discount that possibility on this hand. 0 3

Total possible winners: 2S+3H+3D+3C = 11

An interesting hand, because the safest line is the hardest to spot. The ♣2 will be the fourth highest, so since there are four clubs each with East and West there are no prizes for guessing how many South has. Play the ♣3 and ♣4 on the first trick and let South's singleton win. South is now on lead and with no clubs.

A heart switch sets up the ♥J for a ninth trick.

A spade switch is into the ♠AQ for a ninth trick.

A diamond switch is into the ♦AJ for a ninth trick.

Contract made.

SUIT CONTRACTS

Planning the play in a suit contract is just as important as it is with a NT contract. However, there is a fundamental difference in our approach. It is no longer sensible to start by counting our winners, because more often than not there is a possibility of one or more being ruffed. What you do instead is to first count your losers. This is done by considering just one hand but the high card strength of both. When there are too many you must seek ways in which the number may be reduced, paying special attention to those which could be lost as soon as you lose the lead. Otherwise you should draw trumps and cash your winners. To see exactly how this works we will take you through a few examples.

Firstly a hand which we discussed briefly on page 12.

(N)
7 6 3
K 9 8 6 2
5
A 7 3 2

Bidding:

N	E	S	W
–	–	1H	4C
4H	4S	5H	P
P	P		

(S)
A 5 2
A Q J T 7 3
A 9 6
9

Plan:

Losers: (*using declarer's hand*)

Spades	2
Hearts	0
Diamonds	2
Clubs	0
Total	4

West lead ♣K (two too many)

There is nowhere for the two spades to go, but the ♦96 can be ruffed in dummy after the ♦5 has gone on the ♦A. **Danger:** the opponents' bidding suggests that there are long suits out with shortages opposite. This increases the danger of an immediate ruff by either opponent.

Play: The natural line is to play the ♣A, safely draw trumps, which it is not always possible to do, but which with eleven to two you can comfortably afford here, cross to the ♦A, ruff a diamond, cross to the ♠A, ruff your last diamond, and claim the contract. However, warned by the bidding you should be wary of the ♣A being ruffed, and since it costs nothing you should duck, converting a spade loser into a club loser. What we are saying is that later in the play, having conserved the ♣A, what was previously a spade loser can be thrown on it, the real loser becoming the club nine which you played on the club king. Even with your ducking play you might be defeated, if each opponent is void of partner's suit, and they have one trump each. However, this would require East to make the very good play of ruffing partner's winner in order to return a spade through your ace to get it ruffed.

On page 58 we met this situation:

(W)	(E)					
A K T 9 7 2	Q J	**Bidding:**	N	E	S	W
K 4	A 9 2				–	1S
A 5	K 9 8 7 4 3		P	2D	P	3S
A 9 7	K T		P	4NT	P	5S
			P	5NT	P	6H
			P	7S	P	P
			P			

North lead: ♠3

Plan:

Losers:	Spades	0
(*in West's hand*)	Hearts	0
	Diamonds	0
	Clubs	1
	Total	1 (one too many)

A trump lead is a good lead to make against a grand slam, for it is almost certain to give nothing away, especially against competent opponents. There are two clear lines of play, and there is little to choose between them. You can reckon on the clubs dividing no worse than 6, 2 and aim to ruff the ♣9 with the ♠Q, or you can draw trumps if you think they will be no worse than 3, 2. The division 4, 1 is by no means rare, so probably the ruff is the better line. Let's look at them both.

The club ruff – take the ♠3 with the ♠J, cash the ♣K then the ♣A, and ruff the ♣9 with the ♠Q. Cross to the ♥K, draw trumps, and your hand is good.

Establishment of the diamonds – draw trumps, play ♦A then ♦K and a diamond ruff; cross to the ♥A and ruff another diamond; this should have exhausted the opponent's diamonds, so that when you cross to the ♣K, the ♣9 can be thrown on a diamond, leaving your hand good.

On page 64 we met this situation:

A K T 9 7 2	Q J 8 6 5 3	**Bidding:**	N	E	S	W
K 4	A 2					1S
A 5	7 3		P	4S	P	6S
A 9 7	K T 8		P	P	P	

	Plan:		
	Losers:	Spades	0
North leads ♦Q	(*in West's hand*)	Hearts	0
		Diamonds	1
		Clubs	1
		Total	2 (one too many)

As is usually the case, opponents aim their lead at the Achilles heel. As we pointed out, this is a mirror distribution, so that there are no relative shortages enabling ruffs, nor relatively long suits enabling discards to be set up, but do not despair, follow us down the trail and watch opponents' discomfiture.

Take the ♦Q with the ♦A. Draw trumps. Cash the ♥A and the ♥K, and give up the trick the contract can afford by getting off lead with your remaining diamond.

A T 9 7 2	Q J 8 6 5
–	–
–	–
A 9 7	K T 8

The position is now as shown above. If opponents lead either a diamond or a heart you ruff in one hand and throw your losing club from the other (the famous ruff and discard), and if they return a club you play for the ♣Q and the ♣J to be in different hands. One opponent must play one of the ♣Q and the ♣J or your ♣9 or ♣T will make and your loser is already gone.

Suppose it is North who is on lead, and that the trick goes: N, ♣2; E,♣8; S,♣J; W, ♣A. You now assume the ♣Q to be with North and finesse it through East's ♣KT. Hey presto – except when the wretched clubs are both in one hand of course!

12 Defence

Many players, when they see a hand they regard as 'poorish', switch off and wait for the next hand. They do this again when they have a better hand but have been outbidden by opponents. It is a vicious circle; because they have switched off they do badly and get bored, and then they switch off more. Good players do well even on the poor hands. A moment's thought is all you need to convince yourself. If you succeed in becoming at least a reasonable defender, then you will begin to enjoy all the hands you play instead of only one-third of them. There are several good books around on defence and card play when you have improved enough to want to read them. All we shall do here, therefore, is give you some pointers.

THE OPENING LEAD

Firstly, we cannot stress too strongly that you should listen to the bidding, opponents' as well as partner's, since this is the key to good defence. In particular it will help find a lead. Yet it is evident in general play around the country, from the number of times someone asks 'whose lead is it?', that many 'players' don't listen. There are those who don't even bother to ask, but blithely lead from the wrong hand, giving declarer all kinds of juicy options.

Secondly, if partner has bid a suit, unless you have some very good reason for not doing so (the safest is a void), lead it. It will, of course, sometimes prove to have been the wrong thing to do, but it will tend to keep partner happy, which is never a bad thing. This is called preserving partnership harmony.

Thirdly, if you have an honour sequence of three or more it is rarely an unsafe lead. Examples are: **A** K Q x ; **Q** J T ; **T** 9 8 x.
Otherwise:

A x
J 9 x **x** x
A x x
A x x

V no trumps: If you have enough entries to enjoy use of a long suit such as the one illustrated above once it is established, lead the fourth highest. When, however, you can lead from the top of a solid sequence at the head of a long suit you should do so.

x x
Q x x x x
x x x
x x x

If not, try a short suit (*see* above) in the hope that your shortage represents partner's length, and that the suit can be established. Occasionally, when you suspect that the cards are lying badly for declarer, look for a safe, or neutral lead, one which is not likely to give much, if anything, away.

Q x
x x **x**
J x x x
A Q T 9

V a suit: When it is at all likely that declarer can use dummy's trumps to dispose of losers, and it is safe (for example, not from Qx[x]), lead a trump; the situation where bidding has gone:

N	E	S	W
1H	P	1S	P
2C	P	2H	P

and you have some good club, as in the hand above. From the fact that declarer's partner has given preference it is likely that dummy will be ruffing clubs quite early.

When, on the other hand, you hold a trump or two, and when partner is marked with some values, lead your singleton or doubleton first, hoping to gain a ruff yourself before trumps are drawn. If you choose a lead from length it should again be fourth highest, as *v* NT, when four or more are held, *except* when you have two or more touching honours in the suit, when the highest should be led.

It is important to note this difference in approach when leading from length containing top honours against a suit contract rather than NT. In NT, when you have a long suit, you try to exhaust the opponents' cards in the suit, often giving them one or two 'cheap' tricks initially in order to establish winners for later. Such concession of early tricks is often vital in order to maintain communication with partner. Consider this suit holding: A K 8 7 5.

You:	*(Initial*	A K x/x x	*(Position after one*	A K/x x
Declarer:	*holdings)*	x x Q/	*round of the suit –*	x x
Dummy:		x x x/	*Partner on lead later*	x x
Partner:		x x	*can communicate)*	*x*

First, against a low level NT contract, and assuming your side has done no bidding. There are eight cards out, with a good chance that they will divide 3, 3, 2, and you would do well to suppose partner holds the doubleton. In this case three rounds will exhaust all the holdings except your own, leaving you to cash the last two **provided you are then on lead**. This means AKx need to be played in the other order. After the play of the 7 (fourth highest) from your hand the position is as shown in the second array. Even if partner had a doubleton, the ability to play the remaining card to put you in means you will now make another four tricks in the suit, if or when either of you regains the lead.

Of course, when the distribution is less even, 4, 2, 2 or worse, this ploy may no longer work, although the lead still gives you your best chance of making more than just the AK.

However, in a suit contract it is normally pointless to even try to establish a suit in this way, for even if you do establish winners they are almost certain to be ruffed. Indeed, the lead of the 7 now may well result in you making no tricks in the suit at all, because one opponent could have a singleton Q, or Qx, with declarer able to discard the small card on a winner on another suit in the other hand. So here we lead the ace.

There are many situations where what you play depends not just on your holding, but on what you perceive the situation at the table to be, and the likely distribution of the other cards. Experience will gradually enlighten you.

SIGNALS AND DISCARDS

Both signals and discards give aid during general play. A **signal** is when information is passed to partner via the play of a card of the same suit as the trick in play. A **discard** is, of course, a card of a suit different to that of the suit in play without being a ruff.

Although when dummy is down every player can see half the deal, declarer has an advantage inasmuch as the half seen is coherent, two matching hands. The two hands the defenders see are two separate halves of halves, if you see what we mean. The defenders can develop tools to assist them to overcome the oppositions' advantage, however, principal among which are signals and discards.

The tools must not be a secret code; they must form a system which declarer is entitled under the rules of bridge to know (just like your bidding system). Thus, as the defenders pass information, declarer has the right to be able to interpret what they are saying. For instance, we have seen that when you lead an honour card you will have the next honour to it unless it is a singleton or part of a doubleton. Thus, when you lead A from A *K* Q 7 3, J from J *T* 8, and so on, you give partner (and declarer) information about a *card still in your hand*. You may be wondering, if declarer knows as much as your partner, how you are gaining anything for your trouble. It is because *you choose* what information to pass, and it may well not be what declarer dearly wishes to know.

There are many methods of passing information via signals and discards, and which combination you use is a matter of personal preference and agreement between you and partner. Remember, though, that the rules say you must both use the same system, again as in bidding. The following are some of the more popular.

Encourage / Discourage Signals

In this method, when partner leads a suit, following suit with what appears to be your lowest card implies that for some reason or another you are not keen on partner continuing the suit. To read partner's signal correctly (say the 7 is played on your A) you must look at the cards in your hand and in dummy. If you can see the 2, 3, 4, 6 then partner's 7 is almost certainly 'low', whilst if the only card you can see below 7 is the 3 then the 7 is equally likely now to be 'high'.

If partner's card is unnecessarily high then partner is saying 'I would welcome a continuation partner'. For example, if either you or declarer leads out the AK of a suit, and partner plays first the 7 and then the 2 this is called a 'peter', completed by the play of the 2. There is now no doubt that the 7 was 'high'. There could be several reasons, such as the possession of the Q which is now good, or of a doubleton, so that a continuation could be ruffed. The reason may be more sophisticated than either of these. Partner may not want a damaging switch, or may even want declarer to be made to ruff. Here are some examples:

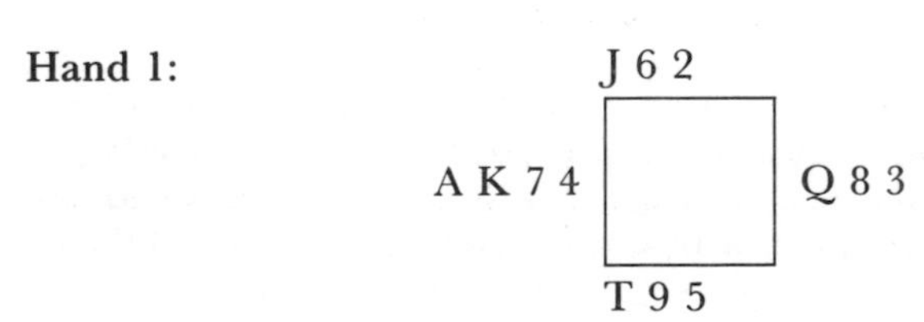

West leads the A and East follows with the 8, indicating that a continuation is welcome. W obliges, and E duly wins the third round.

Hand 2:

Against a trump contract W again leads the A, and again E follows with the 8. W continues with K and another, and E plays the 3 and then gains a ruff.

Hand 3:

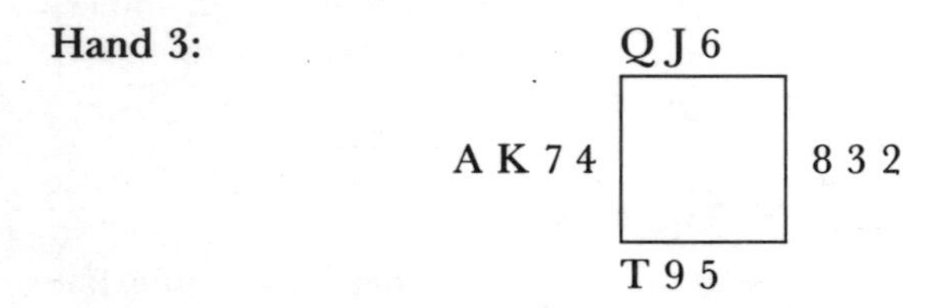

Again W starts with the A. Now E has a choice; if there is another suit E would like led, then play of the 2 might achieve this, whilst if E is worried that a switch could be damaging (say through E's K J to declarer's A Q) then the 8 might be preferred. After all, in most cases declarer is now going to make the Q sometime, so a continuation is not damaging. The continuation in this situation is called **neutral**.

Hand 4:

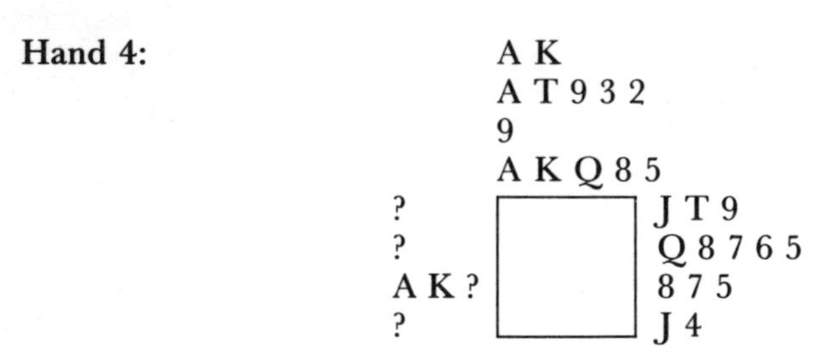

S is in 6S and W leads the ♦A to dummy's singleton 9. E follows with the 8, asking for the continuation. Unless partner has 8 diamonds the contract must now fail, for declarer loses to ♦K as well, or ruffs with the ♠K, after which E's ♠JT9 can only be beaten twice with the A and the Q. One off.

Suit Length Signals

Again, the notable difference between following to a lead with a high or a low card is utilised, this time like this: a high card indicates a holding of even length, 2, 4, 6 . . ., and a low card indicates one of odd length, 1, 3, 5 . . .

On Declarer's Lead

Hand 5:

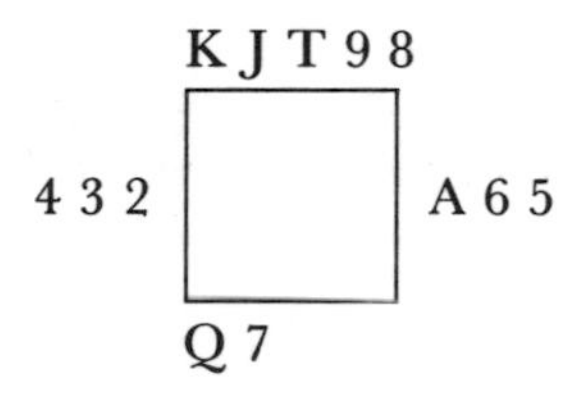

S opens 1NT which is passed out. When dummy goes down its only helpful holding is a five card diamond suit to the KJT. Declarer wins the opening trick and leads the ♦Q to dummy's five card suit. West follows with the 2, the lowest card in the suit. East now knows that partner has an odd number, and can see eight diamond cards. Count: 13–8=5. W cannot have 5 or S could not have led; that means that W either has one or three. If it is one, S has four and there will be nothing E can do, but if W was three . . . Well, then S has 5–3=2, and E may with impunity take the second round with the ace, thus denying S all but the one trick in what is a solid suit between NS, viz: K(Q)JT9.

Hand 6:

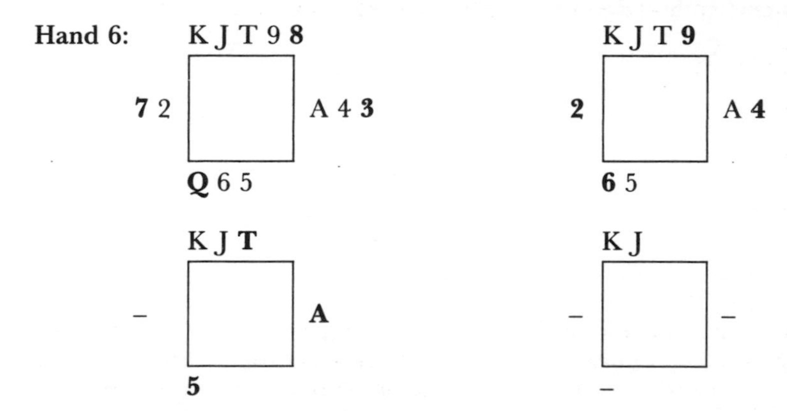

The bidding has gone just as it did in the previous hand, and the opening play is identical too, except that on S lead of ♦Q partner now plays the

7. You can see every card above it, so either partner is singleton or the 7 is high, showing even length. It cannot be four unless S opened 1NT holding a singleton, which is improper, so it should be two; ergo, S holds three diamond cards, and you must hold up your ♦A until the third round to shut S off from dummy, allowing opener two diamond tricks. In either of the above, if you foolishly go up with the A on the first round opener makes four tricks instead of only one or two, as the case may be.

On Partner's Lead

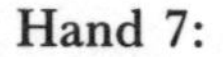

Hand 7:

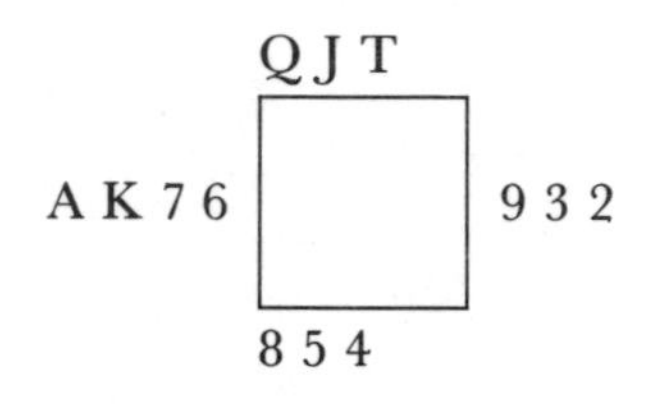

Defending against a NT contract partner leads the A. You follow with the 2, showing odd length. You have 1, 3 or 5, so declarer can be **counted** as 5, 3, or 1, since partner can see 7 cards, leaving you and S to hold 13–7=6. If S has five there is no way of preventing the suit being established, so because there is much more chance of the outstanding six being 3, 3, as indeed they are, partner continues with the K or the 6, depending upon the rest of the hand. If the K is chosen a third card clears the suit, leaving partner with a fourth card established to cash when in again, while the 6 would be preferred if, for instance, partner had no entry other than the K and needed help from you.

Hand 8:

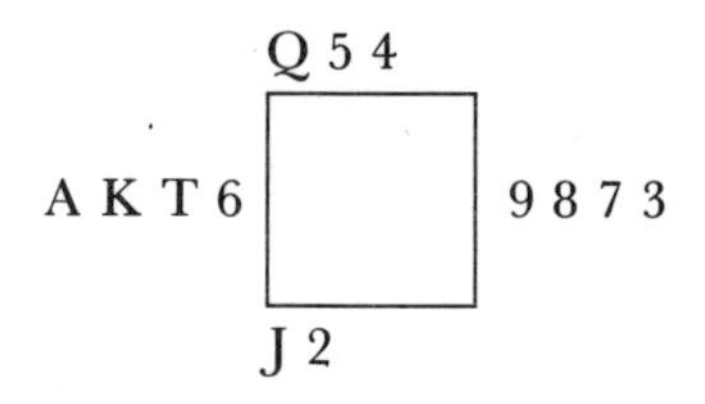

Partner opens the bidding and you raise, but the opposition outbid you in another suit (annoying, but it happens). Partner leads the A and you play the 9. Partner now knows you are 2, 4, 6, with South 4, 2, 0, since partner can see seven cards. You will not be 2, for you raised, and when S follows with the 2 you aren't 6; partner knows now that you are 4 and S is 2. This means that if the suit is continued dummy's Q will become good for a discard to opener, so partner switches.

Hand 9:

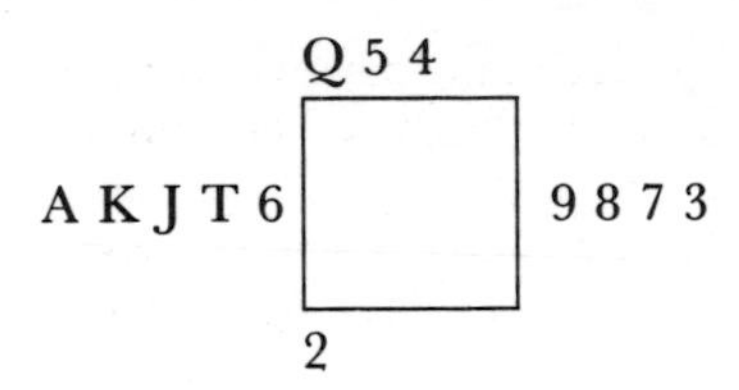

As previously, except that when you now show partner four cards partner knows it would be downright dangerous to continue, for 13–(5+3+4)=1, and that has already gone on the A, so if the K is continued declarer will ruff it and use the Q for a discard later, while on a small card the Q will be played immediately for the discard. If partner switches though there is no damage done from the lead, for whichever card declarer leads from dummy can be covered safely.

Hand 10:

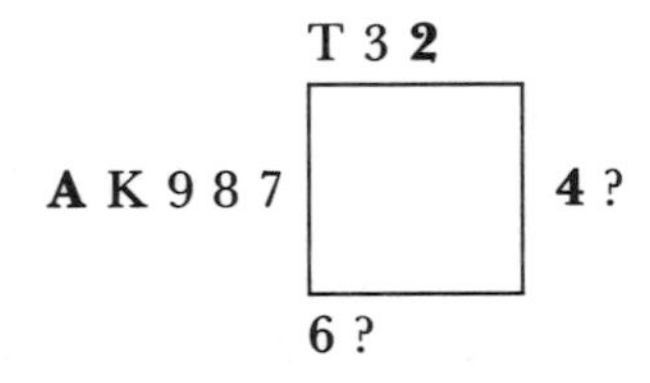

After partner has raised your suit the opponents play the contract in their suit. You lead the A and partner plays the 4. You can see both the 2 and the 3, so the 4 must be low. Partner is odd, 1, 3, 5, leaving declarer to be 4, 2, 0. Partner wouldn't raise on a singleton, so the outstanding cards either split 3, 2 or 5, 0. When the 6 appears you know it is 3, 2 and you can safely play the K. It will not be ruffed, and if partner does not have the Q it will fall from declarer's doubleton, leaving partner's J to cover dummy's T.

Hand 11:

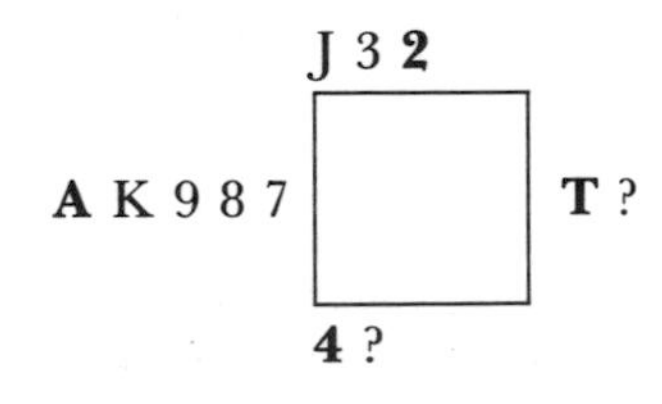

This time partner has passed throughout the auction, and plays the T on your A lead. This has either to be a singleton or high. If it is singleton declarer has four, and the K followed by a small card gives partner a ruff. If it is a doubleton declarer has three, and again the K followed by a small card gives partner a ruff. Lastly, if partner has four declarer is singleton (the 4 already played) and partner has the Q to cover dummy's J. In every case it is safe to continue.

Hand 12:

	K Q 5 4	
	A Q J T 8	
	T	
	T 5 **3**	
A J 2	N	T 9 8 7 6 3
9 4 2	W E	6 5
5 4 3		2
A K Q 6	S	J **9** 7 4
	–	
	K 7 3	
	A K Q J 9 8 7 6	
	8 2	

South is declarer in 6D, and W leads the ♣A, to which partner follows with the 9. When declarer plays the 8, how many players would switch to the ♠A? As you can see, if you do it is a disaster, for your A is ruffed, and later declarer will be able to throw the losing ♣on either of the ♠K or a ♥. Of course, you knowing now how to count, knew it was safe to cash the ♣K.

Which technique should you use, given the choice? Well, let's compare encourage/discourage signals with suit length signals, both after partner has led.

Encourage/discourage signals: It is easy to remember. High encourages, low discourages. HELD. On the other hand it involves judgement on the part of the signaller as to whether to encourage or discourage, and mistakes can be made.

Suit length signals: No judgement is involved, simply factual information, and for this reason it is preferred by more experienced players. On the other hand, it is of no earthly use until you can count reliably and then assess the complete hand with confidence and accuracy, so at the moment you would probably be advised to stick with the previous option, transferring your allegiance only when you feel confident that you can cope with the detail involved.

Encourage/Discourage Discards

In the same way that the play of a high or low card in following partner's lead encourages or discourages continuation of the suit led, so the discard of a high or low card of a particular suit encourages or discourages a switch to the suit from which the discard was made. For example:

holding K Q J 8 2 discard the 8

holding 852 discard the 2.

This method has the advantage of simplicity, together with conformity if you adopt HELD. Here is an example of the method in use:

Hand 13:

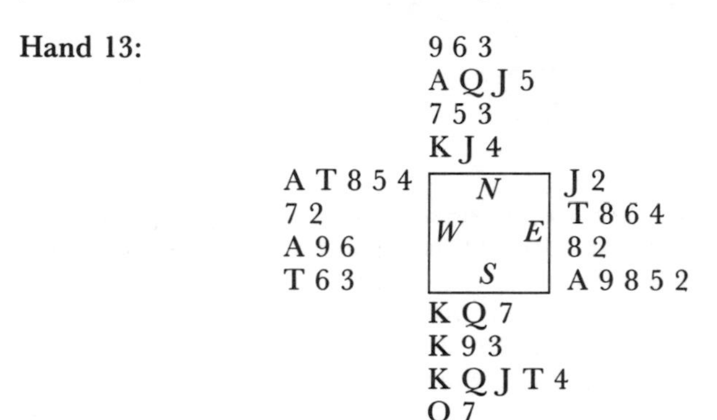

South is declarer in 3NT and W leads the ♠5, fourth highest. Declarer plays the 3 from dummy, and E plays J, losing to the K. The spades are now:

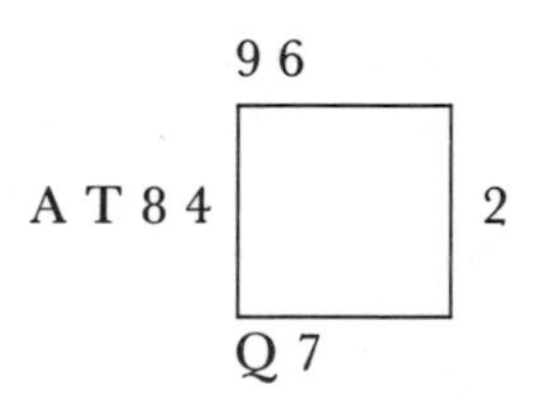

S plays the ♦K, and W holds off, N playing the 3 and E the 8. S continues with the ♦Q and W still holds up, N playing the 6 and E the 2. The peter is complete, and W knows partner had two and will be able to pass information on the next trick via a discard. ♦ JA7 follow, and E discards the ♣9 to encourage a lead to the A. Note that the ♥4 to discourage a heart might not work, since partner might switch to a spade (E could hold the ♠Q; the standard play from QJ2 is the J).

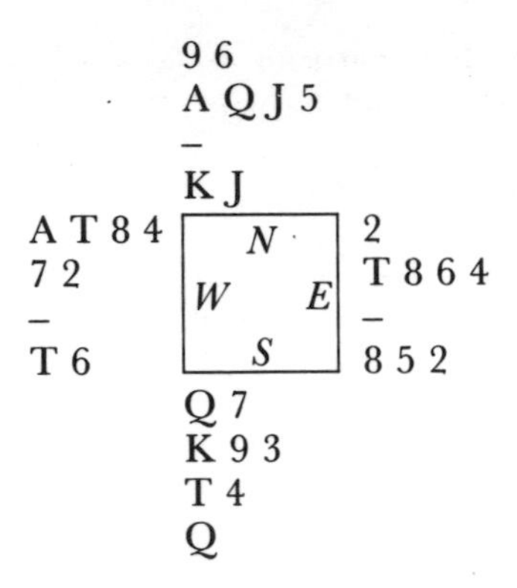

When a club is led, 3, 4, A, 7 the situation is as above: your side has won the ♦A and the ♣A, 2 tricks. Declarer has won the ♠K, ♦K, and ♦Q. If E leads a heart or club declarer wins in hand, cashes two diamonds and throws the spades from table. If a club was led the ♥K is cashed, and dummy is good for the remainder of the tricks. Plus two. But E remembers partner's spade lead and plays the 2, giving partner 4 spade tricks. Two off.

It was in order to lead spades through declarer that E signalled the club entry, and that W held off with the ♦A until E could signal. Note the attempt by declarer to entice W into switching to a ♠ by playing the ♠K, so that W doesn't know who has the ♠Q, partner or declarer. That is why the ♣9 is necessary.

The disadvantage of the method is the loss of a card which could win a trick if you still held it later in the play of the hand.

Length-Showing Discards

These are used by many leading players, but the inferences to be drawn require thought even by very experienced players, and the process of drawing them can be so complex that we do not propose to discuss the method at this stage.

Suit Preference Discards in the Style of Lavinthal or McKenney

When you have to discard on a suit in NT, or on trumps in a trump contract, because you are void in that suit or the trump suit, there are three remaining suits in your hand. You select the suit in which you have least interest, and that leaves two. These two will have relative rankings, one being higher than the other. If your principal interest is in the higher ranking of the two you throw a highish card from your no interest suit, and if it is in the lower of the two you throw a low card. Look again at hand 13:

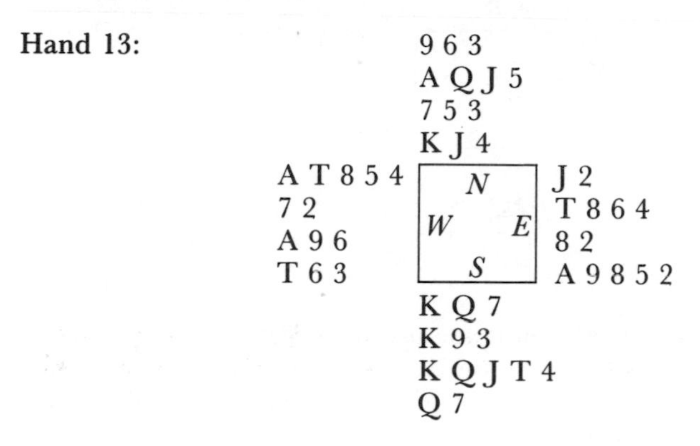

Bidding:	S	N
	1D	1H
	1NT	3NT
	P	

S is playing in 3NT as before, and again W leads ♠5 (fourth highest). Again declarer sets out to establish the diamond suit, and again W holds off until the third round to allow E to make a helpful discard. This time, wanting a club switch so that the ♠2 can be led, E discards a heart. Clubs being lower ranking than spades the ♥4 is thrown. This says, 'I have no diamonds, and am not interested in hearts; I want the lower ranking of the other two (a club).'

Discards in the Revolving Style

The discard of a low card asks for the first suit held below the suit from which the discard has come, and the discard of a high card asks for the first suit held above the discard suit (discounting the void suit, of course). The term 'revolving' comes from the use made of the ranking 'cycle'. Thus, in a NT contract by South your partner leads C6 which runs round to declarer's Q. Declarer now leads AKQ of hearts, you having started with a doubleton heart. The situation is now this:

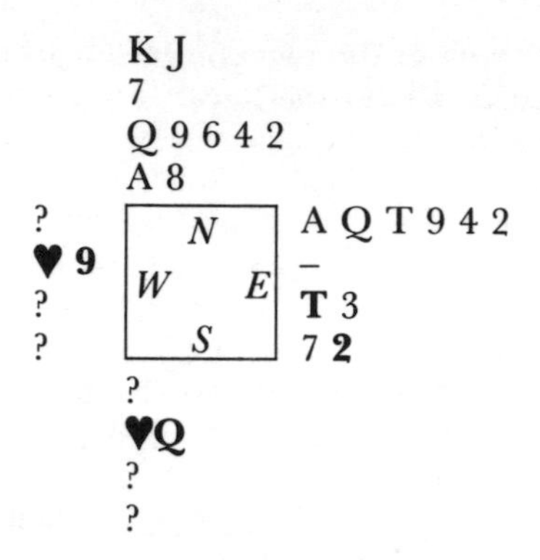

Partner follows with the ♥9, and dummy with ♥7. Maybe partner is going to get in with ♦K when declarer tries to establish dummy's diamonds. If so, a spade switch from partner at that stage will present you with six tricks. On this occasion you have two choices:

♦T = suit 'above' = spades;
♣2 = suit 'below' = spades.

The Ruffing McKenney Signal

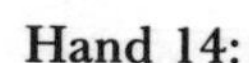
Hand 14:

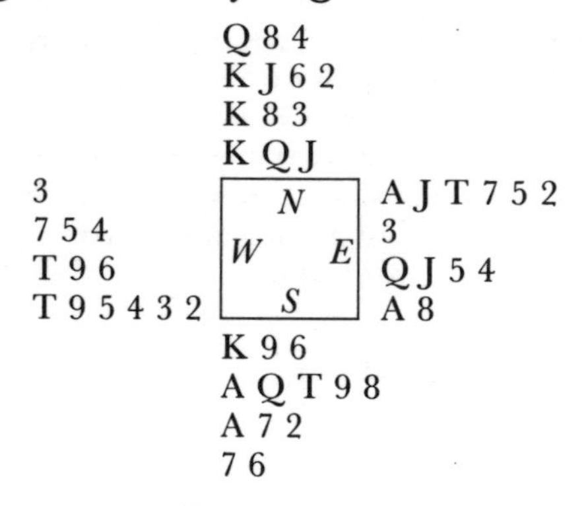

Sitting W you hear partner open 1S, S overcall with 2H, and N raise to 4H. You lead the ♠3 and partner wins with the A and continued with the ♠2. You ruff with the ♥4 and wonder.

Well, you shouldn't. Partner has led the ♠2 from a long suit, and could easily have chosen a high card. The ♠2 is *low*, and says, 'I want a *low* ranking return.' Since hearts are not a likely switch you are being told how to choose between clubs and diamonds. *Low* = a club. Sure enough, partner wins with ♣A and gives you another ruff. One down.

If you'd had to guess and had led a diamond, declarer would have won and drawn trumps, making the contract. Now let's rearrange the hand slightly:

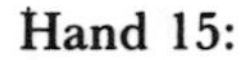

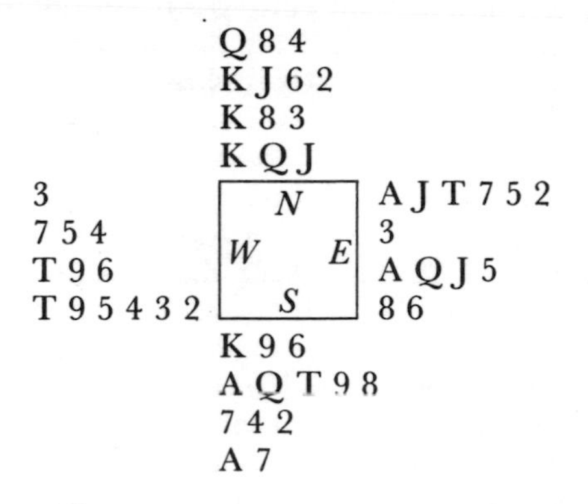

Assume the same bidding, final contract, and opening lead of the ♠3. Now after some thought partner returns ♠J for the ruff. This is saying: 'Partner, I want the *higher* ranking of the other two suits (a diamond).' Note that the diamond return, followed by another spade ruff, the ♠T saying to continue with diamonds, ends with you taking ♠A, ♠ruff, diamond, ♠ruff, and two diamonds; three off.

If you make the mistake of returning a club, declarer wins, draws trumps, discards a diamond on a club, and loses ♠A, ♠ruff, and two diamonds; only one off.

The McKenney Signal in NT

Hand 16:

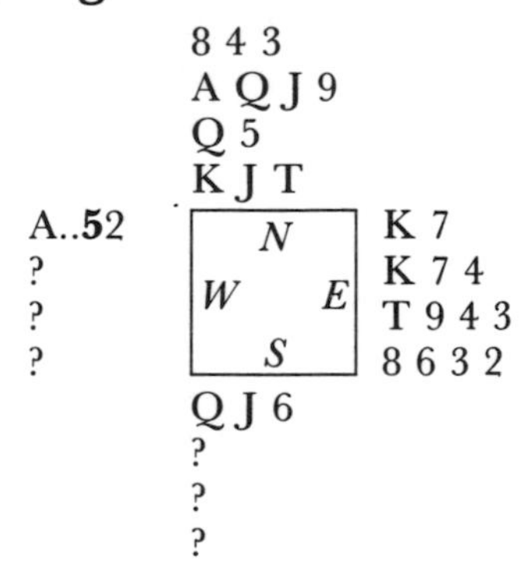

The contract is 3NT by South, and partner leads the ♠5 (fourth highest). You take with the ♠K and return the ♠7. Partner wins with the ♠A and continues with the ♠2. This gives you your clue; when you are in with the ♥K you don't need to guess. That is fortunate, because looking at dummy and left to your own devices you would have been likely to lead a diamond in the hope of getting partner back in. However, the ♠2 is *low*, so you switch to a club. Note that partner could signal for any of the other three suits. After the ♠K and ♠A have been made you have seen:

K 6 **5** 3 on trick 1,
A J **7** 4 on trick 2,
Q 8 from NS on trick 3; this means that partner had to chose from T 9 **2** to lead to trick 3.

Technically, the lead of ♠T would have asked for a heart, ♠9 for a diamond, and in fact ♠2 asked for a club. So you see, you would have known, wherever partner's entry was.

In this particular hand, however, with the heart holding in dummy, there could be no conceivable reason for a heart lead into dummy, so the ♠T would also be asking for a diamond. The complete deal is:

	8 4 3 A Q J 9 Q 5 K J T	
A T 9 5 2 8 3 2 8 2 A 9 7	*N* *W* *E* *S*	K 7 K 7 4 T 9 4 3 8 6 3 2
	Q J 6 T 6 5 A K J 7 6 Q 5	

This is by no means all there is to be said, but it's enough for now.

13 Joining a Club

If you cannot discover locally where bridge is played you should get in touch with the English Bridge Union (EBU), Broadfields, Bicester Road, Aylesbury, Buckinghamshire, HP19 3BG (telephone: 0296 394414).

Every club in the country should be affiliated to them, so they will be able to tell you where the clubs in your neighbourhood are, and provide you with details of club secretaries whom you can contact. There should also be local sources of information. Try the Citizens' Advice Bureau. They will be likely to know all the registered recreational facilities in the area, including bridge clubs. If you cannot get hold of their telephone number, your local town hall may be able to help.

Another source of information is the local press. They may publish club results, amongst other things, and whether they do or not they are likely to know what clubs exist and how to get in touch with them.

Usually, through one or other of the above sources, you can obtain the name, address and telephone number of the secretary of each functioning club. The thing to do then is to ring the secretary and find out: where they meet; when they meet; their attitude to new members; their willingness to arrange a partner for you if you don't already have one; the conditions of membership (price, for instance); the best night to start.

There may be another useful local resource available. There may well be a further education bridge class, and either the local education authority themselves or one of their lecturers may know about local club facilities.

If the local club would prefer you to join with a partner, and there are local classes, one way of going about it is to enrol in such a class and 'eye' the other members, propositioning one when the scene is clear.

The club will be run by a committee of the members, who will decide the forms in which competition will take place locally. They will not decide the rules; these are decided, as in football and cricket, by the national association, in this case the aforementioned EBU.

Clubs come in various shapes and sizes. We have played in a great many clubs and not found two alike. All you can do is to go along and judge the situation for yourself. Above all, don't be afraid – have a go. And if you feel unsure about joining a new club, remember that it is always easier to penetrate somewhere new with moral support – such as the partner 'discovered' at a bridge class, as suggested above.

14 Duplicate Play and Scoring

In competitive play, however informal, the deals are 'stored' in **boards** or wallets, numbered from 1 to 32. There are four slots or pockets which will just accommodate thirteen cards. The boards are sometimes predealt, but are more often dealt at the table at the commencement of play. The four pockets are labelled N, E, S, W, and an indication is given, often by a red label, when NS or EW or both are to be treated as vulnerable. The dealer is shown. Most boards or wallets have a slot provided for a travelling score sheet. If an inexpensive type is in use this may be missing, when it is usual to tuck the folded 'traveller' in with North's hand.

When the deal has been played, North, East, South and West each carefully put their cards in the pocket labelled for them, face down. Remember, in order to do this you keep your cards in front of you as each is played, as we showed you on page 8. It is courteous to 'shuffle' the cards before replacing them. This serves two purposes. The order in which the cards have been played at your table is concealed, and the player taking them out at the table where they are next played has a hand presenting a random appearance, as if it had just been dealt. Most players prefer to meet each new hand in this way – their first assessment is often made as they sort it.

Pairs and boards circulate around the room in a predetermined fashion, arranged so that no two pairs play each other twice and no pair plays the same board twice. The result of the play at each table is recorded on a score sheet which travels with the board. Several pairs play each hand (hence the name **duplicate**) and the performances of those sitting the same way can be compared by means of the score sheet. The element of luck present in any short rubber bridge session is thus largely eliminated, although of course you and the others playing 'your way' may find a run of poor hands where you spend your time defending.

BIDDING BOARDS

These come in various designs, and are used in many clubs. Because they prevent other players from overhearing the bidding at some other table and remembering it to their advantage, they are sometimes called silent bidders. They have all the various calls or components of calls marked on them, and you 'call' by pointing to, and touching clearly, the components of your call.

CONTROL OF A COMPETITIVE BRIDGE SESSION

Control is in the hands of a **Director**, who:
- sets out the table numbers and any movement cards;
- ensures that there are boards to play; and
- arbitrates in the case of any dispute or query at the table, using the handbook of EBU regulations.

If you require the director for any reason whatsoever, you put up your hand, call 'Director' clearly, and keep your hand raised until that person arrives.

When this happens, there has usually been an infringement of the rules, and the director has then to give a ruling.

SITTING NORTH

It is the responsibility of North to:
- procure the right boards for the round, or check that the right boards have been put on the table by the director;
- check that the right EW pair are present for the round;
- place each board correctly aligned NESW before the hands are removed;
- place each board correctly for the hands to be replaced; and
- complete the travelling score sheets and replace them.

The opposition should be invited to check the completed traveller before it is replaced in the board. The other players at the table have a responsibility to check for themselves. If any mistake occurs which damages the movement, or the play of a board elsewhere in the room, both pairs at the table of origin of the mistake are penalised equally.

It follows that, given a choice, as in a Mitchell movement, when you first go to a club you should aim to sit EW and observe. If the movement is a Howell, the pair sitting EW when you are N will, if you point out your inexperience, make sure that you do the right things. Until you are confident, do this. There is no point in sitting there sweating in case you do something wrong. There is no sin in inexperience – we all have to start at some time. It is unwise to pretend, and so get yourself into a mess which then has to be sorted out by others.

BRIDGE MOVEMENTS

The way in which the boards and the players move around the room, arranged so that as many pairs as possible for the number present play each hand, is called 'the movement', and for pairs play this is either a **Mitchell** movement or a **Howell** movement. The tables in play are numbered for this purpose.

Each time you sit down and play two or more boards at a table you have played a **round**. You might play a twenty-four board session in twelve two-board rounds, eight three-board rounds, or six four-board rounds. Remember, you play against fresh opponents in each round. The boards for a round are called a set.

Mitchell Movements

In a room with a large number of players a Mitchell movement is used. All the NS pairs stay seated, and only the EW pairs move. If you are seated NS in such a movement you are competing with all the other NS pairs in the room, although you are playing against the EW pairs. There will usually be two different result lists, all the NS pairs being on one list, and all the EW pairs on the other.

In the simplest form of the movement EW pairs move 'up' (from table six to table seven, for instance) or 'down'. This decision is declared at the beginning of the session by the director. The boards move in the opposite direction. In this movement NS meet pairs in one order, one by one, and sets of boards in the other order, one by one. EW meet NS pairs one by one, and boards by alternate sets.

Howell Movements

In a full Howell movement every pair plays every other pair. In a three-quarter Howell each pair plays a patterned selection of three-quarters of the rest of the room. There is enough mathematical intersection for there to be a fair statistical comparison. In Howell movements, as you progress around the room, you are likely to sit at a table more than once, and you will sit EW and NS at different times.

Movement Cards for a Howell

The moves you have to make in this 'dance around the room' are revealed by means of movement cards on each table. Each card will carry the table number at the top, and somewhere on the card will be an instruction for each pair so that they know where to go at the end of the round. The card will have a line for each round, stating which pair numbers should be sitting NS and EW during that round, and which number boards should be in play between them during that round. For example:

3/4 Howell			**Table 4**
Round	**NS**	**EW**	**Boards**
1	3	7	7, 8, 9
2	4	8	10, 11, 12
3	5	9	13, 14, 15
4	6	10	16, 17, 18
5	7	11	19, 20, 21
6	8	12	22, 23, 24
7	9	1	1, 2, 3
8	10	2	4, 5, 6

NS go to 5 EW
EW go to 1 EW

DUPLICATE BRIDGE SCORING

This is the same as for rubber bridge, except for the following: there are no rubbers and so no rubber bonuses; each board is scored as an independent unit; and games and part scores are given bonuses instead.

		NV	V
	Part score	50	50
	Game	300	500
Undertricks doubled:	first	100	
	next two	200	
	subsequent	300	

Bonus for a redoubled contract made = 100

Undertricks doubled is a most important change, introduced to discourage absurdly cheap sacrifices against V slams.

RUBBER BRIDGE SCORING

Contracted tricks made which score **below the line:**

			Doubled	Redoubled
C/D tricks		20	40	80
H/S tricks		30	60	120
NT tricks	first	40	80	160
	each subsequent	30	60	120

Scores which go **above the line:**

		NV	V	NV	V	NV	V
overtricks		trick	value	100	200	200	400
undertricks	first trick	50	100	100	200	200	400
each subsequent trick		50	100	200	300	400	600

Bonuses:

small slam	500	750
grand slam	1,000	1,500

Insult for made contract X or XX:	50
Rubber won two games to one:	500
Won two games to nil:	700
Single game in an abandoned rubber:	300
Part-score in an abandoned rubber:	50

SCORING A BOARD – MATCH POINTS

At the end of a duplicate session the performance of each pair is calculated relative to the other pairs playing the same boards the same way. This is normally done by match pointing (MP) the results. On each board the pairs playing it are awarded 2MP for every opposing pair they beat, and 1MP for each pair they tie with.

Use of the formula 2x(n–1) gives the highest score to be awarded on a board played n times. **2x4=8 is the top on a board played five times**, as in our example below. This is the score you would get for beating every other pair your way, four of them.

At the end of the session the match points scored by each pair are totalled, usually on a master sheet, and are then either announced by the director or published as soon as possible on the club notice board.

As an example, consider the following deal. For our purposes in this exercise all we want is the completed score sheet at the end of the session. It is a Howell movement, with each board played five times. NS are vulnerable, and N dealt.

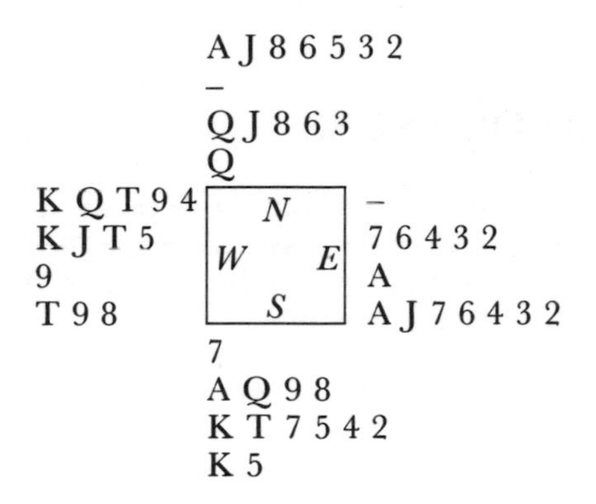

NS	EW	Contract	By	NS+	NS–	NSMP	EWMP
1							2
2	7	2SX+1	N	870		8	
3	1	5D	S	600		6	
4							6
5	4	5D–1	S		100	2	
6	10	5CX	E		550	0	
7							0
8	9	4HX–1	W	100		4	
9							4
10							8

Appendix A
Problems in Bidding

BIDDING SEQUENCES

This appendix involves a preliminary exercise in logic. The hands displayed at the end of Chapter 2 are taken from five deals at the table. Taken in a certain logical order they fall back into those separate deals. Sort out which set of four is which.

Now match each set of four hands alphabetically with the positions NESW. Then put the 'boards', or 'deals', in order thus: label the one containing hand A as deal 1; of the hands remaining place the one containing the earliest alphabetically labelled hand as deal 2. Continue like this until you have laid out and labelled all five deals.

Construct what you think would be the likely bidding sequences on each hand, with N dealer on each occasion.

CALLS

1 What would be your call as dealer if the hand you saw was:

(a)	(b)	(c)	(d)
A T 9 7 6 3	A J 3	5	A K Q 5
8 3	A J 7 3	A T 7 2	Q 8 7
A 8 5 4	J 7 5	Q J 9 7	–
A	A 3 2	K Q J 9	A 9 8 6 3 2

(e)	(f)	(g)	(h)
K 2	Q 9 5	K 8 3	A Q 6 4
T 5 3	K J T	K Q J T 5	K 7
K Q 9 8 7 5 2	K Q 9 6	A K	K 8 7 6 3
J	T 4 2	A Q 7	4 3

(k)	(m)	(n)	(p)
K Q 6	A 9 6	A K Q 8 2	K 8 6
A K 9	A K 9 4 3	A K J 7 3	T 2
9 7 6	J 9 7 6 4	K 2	A Q 8 6
A 4 3 2	–	8	A Q J T

2 What action would you take on each of the following hands if dealer on your right had opened:

		(a)	(b)	(c)	(d)
A	1C	Q 8 2	A K 9 7 5 4	K 9 5	Q J 4 3
B	1D	A K 8 6 4	K T 3	6	K J 4 2
C	1S	A Q 8 6	Q J 9	A J T 4 3	K J 8 6
D	1NT	7	8	A Q 9 5	5
E	2H				

3 Partner opens 1H and the next hand passes. What action would you take holding:

(a)	(b)	(c)	(d)	(e)
A 2	T 3	K Q 4	A T 6	Q 8 4
T 9 3 2	9 5	8 4	–	9 7 2
A K J	A 8 4 3	A 8 4	K J T 5 3	A J 3
Q J 5 4	K J 5 3 2	A K Q 5 4	K T 6 4 3	K J 9 6

Appendix B Answers

CHAPTERS 1 TO 14

Page 19

	1	2	3	4
A	**9**/11	S–, H–, D++	no	2D
	(**9** high card points, +2 for length if the hand is played in D)			
B	5	S–	no	Pass
C	8	H–	no	1NT
D	7/8	H+, D–	no	2H
E	7/8	S+, H––	no	1S
F	15/17	S––, H–, C++	yes, 1C	2C
G	16/20	H++++, D–––, C–	yes, 2H	3C (a forcing bid has to be found)
H	17/18	S+, D–	yes, 1S	2S
J	11/12	D––, C+	yes, 1C	2C
K	5/7	S++, D–, C––	no	1S
L	2	C–	no	Pass
M	3/4	S––, D+	no	Pass
N	9/10	H–, D+, C–	no	1S
P	12	none	no	2NT
Q	18	S–	yes, 1H	3C
R	14	H–	yes, 1NT	3NT
S	16	none	yes, 1C	2C
T	7/8	H+, D–, C–	no	3H
U	12/13	S+, H–, C–	yes, 1S	1S
V	7	S–	no	1NT

Page 25

9
K J 7 4
A T 6 5
A J 9 7
50

You misguidedly open 1C and partner responds with 1S. If you rebid your clubs partner will 'know' that you have five of them. If you rebid 1NT partner will 'know' you have sixteen to eighteen points. If you rebid in either diamonds or hearts partner will 'know' that you are strong enough to reverse, and that you have five clubs!

Page 76

96	2S	Not a lot to spare.
97	2D	Don't be tempted into passing because of the six clubs and the poor hand.
98	2D	Don't bid 2H, you aren't good enough. You can show them later.
99	4D	The solid suit. You have to jump because 2D is the negative and 3D is only a normal positive.
100	3NT	If the diamonds were better the response would be 3D.
101	2H	Not ideal, but you must give a positive response, and this is the best one.
102	2NT	Eight to ten balanced. In hand 100 there were eleven.
103	3C	The bare minimum, but a five card suit headed by the AK is always worth a positive.

Page 80

105 11 **106** 8½ **107** 8 **108** 8 **109** 9

Page 81

110 2NT, 4H, 4S **111** 3C, 3C, 3C **112** 2S, 3NT, 4S
113 2H, 3H, 2NT

111 2, 3 It is tempting to support partner immediately, but that can come later, while if you don't show your C now you never will.

112 1 2S not 4D, because that takes you past 3NT.
2 Ideal for 3NT.
3 A bit good for 4S, but has no alternative. Will accept any slam invitation.

113 1,3 The H are good enough to show at the 2 level, but not at the 3 level.

Page 112

	You		Missing		
♠	A	= 4	K+Q+J	= 6	
♥	K	= 3	Q+J	= 3	A = 4
♦	K+Q+J	= 6			A = 4
♣	K	= 3	Q+J	= 3	A = 4
Totals		16		12	12

But partner is known to hold between 13 and 15 points, and without at least one ace can only reach a count of twelve. Partner holds at least one ace and will not bid 4D.

Partner's small diamonds having been thrown on your hearts, it will be ruffed. It is true, by the way, that if partner has only four spades and they break badly the slam may not be on, but the odds are in your favour. With the trumps 4,1 you still have a chance: partner may have ♣A or ♦Q, or opponents may lead ♣A for a ruff and partner hold ♣K.

Page 125

Contract: 6NT by West Lead ♦4

The spades offer the only two way communication,

Q 4	A K J 5	= Q 4	v	5 J K A	= 4 and a blockable suit
K Q 5 4	A J	= 5 4 Q K	v	A J	= 4 A blocked suit.
A 9 7 6 5	T 8 2	= A			= 1 A vulnerable suit.
K Q	A 9 7 6	= K Q	v	6 7 A	= 3 A blocked suit.

Take ♦A, play off ♣KQ, and cross ♥J with ♥4 leaving:

Q 4	A K J 5	
K Q 5	A	
9 7 6 5	T 8	Cash ♥A, ♣A throwing a diamond, cross to
–	A 9	the ♠Q with ♠5 leaving:

4	A K J	
K Q	–	
9 7 6	T 8	Cash ♥KQ throwing 2 diamonds, cross to
–	9	the ♠J with the ♠4 leaving:

–	A K	
–	–	
9 7 6	–	
–	9	Cash ♠AK, throwing 2 diamonds.

Give them the thirteenth trick, containing your ♦9+♣9.

♦A, ♣K, ♣Q, ♥J, ♥A, ♣A, ♠Q, ♥K, ♥Q, ♠J, ♠A, ♠K = 12 tricks

APPENDIX A

Bidding Sequences

Deal 1

		(A)	K 5 T 3 A Q T 9 8 3 6 5 4
(G)	J 8 6 A K J 8 7 6 4 2 – A K	*N* *W* *E* *S*	(C) Q 9 3 Q 5 K 7 5 2 J 8 3 2
		(E)	A T 7 4 2 9 J 6 4 Q T 9 7

N	E	S	W
P	P	P	2H
P	2NT	P	4H
P	P	P	

Deal 2

		(B)	T 8 J 9 7 J T 9 7 K 7 3 2
(U)	A J 7 6 2 Q 5 K Q 8 5 9 4	*N* *W* *E* *S*	(D) 9 4 3 A K T 8 3 6 2 T 8 6
		(S)	K Q 5 6 4 2 A 4 3 A Q J 5

N	E	S	W
P	P	1C	1S
2C	2S	3C	P
P	P		

Note how, with twenty-one points and a flat hand opposite a flattish hand, the contract goes two off, while with only nineteen high card points but distribution, EW can make 3S as the cards lie.

Deal 3

```
                 2
            (F)  Q 7
                 A K 5 2
                 A Q T 9 8 5
        9                        K Q 7 6 3
   (M)  J T 6 5     N       (H)  A K 2
        Q T 6 4 3  W   E         J 9
        4 3 2       S            K J 6
                 A J T 8 5 4
            (K)  9 8 4 3
                 8 7
                 7
```

N	E	S	W
1C	1NT	P	2D
P	P	2S	P
P	P		

Deal 4

```
                 K Q 5 3
            (J)  Q 8 7
                 8
                 K J 7 6 5
        J 8                      9 7 6
   (Q)  A K T 6     N       (L)  J 4 3 2
        A 7 4      W   E         J 6 5 2
        A Q T 2     S            9 3
                 A T 4 2
            (N)  9 5
                 K Q T 9 3
                 8 4
```

N	E	S	W
P	P	P	1H
P	P	P	

Deal 5

	(P) A T 9 5 7 6 4 K T 8 A J 3	
(V) J 2 A J 3 J 5 4 3 9 6 5 4	*N* *W* *E* *S*	(R) K 8 7 9 8 A Q 9 2 K Q 8 7
	(T) Q 6 4 3 K Q T 5 2 7 6 T 2	

N	E	S	W
P	1NT	P	P
P			

Calls

1 (a) 12 HCP and a six card suit: 1S.
(b) 15 HCP and a balanced hand: 1NT.
(c) 13 HCP, 4, 4, 4, 1: 1H, the suit below the singleton.
(d) 15 HCP and 6, 4: 1C, the longer suit.
(e) 8 HCP without the ♣J, and a seven card suit to the KQ. NV open 3D, otherwise pass.
(f) 11 HCP and a balanced hand: Pass.
(g) The hand has the qualifications for: 2NT 22 HCP, balanced, and
2H ½S+4H+2D+1½C=8 playing tricks.

We prefer 2NT, but either is correct, being a matter of style.
(h) 12 HCP, and only a poor five card suit: Pass.
(k) 16 HCP, too many for 1NT although the hand is balanced: 1C.
(m) 12 HCP, and you will be unlucky not to find partner with either heart or diamond support; furthermore, the heart suit is good: 1H.
(n) 4S+3½H+½D= 8 playing tricks: 2S.
(p) 16 HCP, too many for 1NT although the hand is balanced. There are two touching suits; bid the higher: 1D.

2 (a) A Overcall 1H. A double for take out is a good alternative.
B 1H.
C 2H.

D Most modern players would double, but if the singleton C worries you, by all means bid 2H.

E To have eight playing tricks opener must have six or seven H to the QJT, and solid top honours in S and C. Pass, and hope they get into trouble.

(b) A, B 1S. C Pass. D, E 2S.

(c) A, B Pass. C, D 2D. E NV, double for take out; V, pass.

(d) A Double for take out at favourable vulnerability. B, C, D, E Pass.

3 (a) Raise to 4H.

(b) Bid 1NT; there is not enough to bid at the two level.

(c) Bid 3C; a jump in a new suit is forcing, showing a powerful hand; there may well be a slam on.

(d) Bid 2D; if partner rebids hearts you will have an awkward decision to make; the best alternative then is probably to bid 3C.

(e) Bid 2NT, showing eleven or twelve points and a balanced/semi balanced hand without four hearts.

Appendix C
Hands used in the Text

These are organised as follows:

The interplay hands used in Chapter 5 are listed first, even if they occurred earlier in the text. They are in two sections, opening hands and responding hands. Then all other hands in the book starting at Chapter 2 are listed in the order in which they appear.
The first bracketed number to the left of the top of a hand indicates the page on which it first appears in the book, whilst other pages on which it appears are chronicled at the foot of each hand.

CHAPTER 5

1NT Openings

(21)	K 9 7	A K	K T 9 2	A T 9 7	A T 9
	J 8	K J 7	Q J 7	K J 7	K J 8 7
	A J 6 5	J 6 5	A J	A T 5	T 6 5 2
	A J 9 5	J 9 7 5 3	Q J 5 3	J 9 5	A Q
	11	**12**	**14**	**15**	**16**
	(52) (57)	(32) (46)	(27) (46)	(46) (51)	(32) (46)
	(63) (70)	(62) (66)	(60) (67)		(52) (57)
		(69) (31)	(70)		(31)

A T 7	(30)	A K T 2	(34)	T 9	(46)	A T 7 2
K Q 7 4		K 8 7 4		K J 7 4		K J 8 7
J 5		A T		A J 6		A 6
A J 5 3		9 7 5		A J 9 7		J 9 5
17		**55**		**66**		**81**
(27) (49)		(46) (65)		(51) (50)		(63) (67)
(55) (58)		(68)		(56) (64)		(72)
(66)						

1S Openings

(22)	A T 9 7	A K T 2	(23)	A K T 9 7 2	A K T 7 2	K T 9 7 2
	K 7 4	K 8		K 4	–	K J 7 4 3
	A T 6	J T 6 5		A 5	A J T 6 5	A J 5
	A J 3	A Q J		A 9 7	A 5 3	–
	18	**24**		**33**	**41**	**43**
	(45) (53) (57)	(44) (56) (61) (70)		(48) (58) (64) (108) (130) (131)	(25) (48) (45) (49) (62)	(52) (59) (68)

	K T 9 7 2	(44)	A K 9 7 2	(56)	A T 9 7 2	(55)	A T 9 7 2
	–		K J 8		8		K Q 7
	A J T 6		J 6		A J T		6
	A Q J 9		A J 7		A J 7 3		A J 5 3
	47		**78**		**83**		**84**
	(51) (65) (69)		(63) (66)		(56) (61)		(67) (71)

1H Openings

(22)	K T 7	A T 9 7	(23)	A 7	T 9	2
	K 8 4 3	K Q 8 4		K J 8 7 4	K J 8 7 4	K J 7 4 3
	A J 5	A T		J T 6	A J T 2	A 5
	A Q 5	A 9 3		A 7 5	A 9	A J 9 7 3
	19	**25**		**32**	**38**	**42**
	(44) (53) (67)	(45) (59) (68)		(48) (56) (58) (61)	(49) (53) (63)	(25) (54) (64) (66)

(25)	9	(25)	A T 9 2	(45)	K T 9 7	(49)	A K T 9
	K J 7 4		K Q 7 4		K J 8 7 4 3		K J 8 7 4
	A T 6 5		A J T 5		A J		T
	A J 9 7		J		7		A 9 5
	50		**51**		**79**		**82**
	(50) (55) (65) (69)		(51) (53) (62)		(45) (48) (70)		(57) (64) (71)

1D Openings

(22)	A 9 2	A K T	K 7	(23)	K T 7	A
	K J 4	K J	K J 7		8	J 8 7 4
	A J 6 5	A T 6 5	A J T 5		A J T 6 5 2	A J T 6 5
	A J 3	J 9 7 3	A J 9 5		A J 3	A Q J
	20	**22**	**23**		**34**	**44**
	(55) (66)	(49) (62)	(54) (59)		(45) (51)	(50) (53)
		(68)	(65) (70)		(53) (61)	(61) (71)

K T 9 7	A	(25)	A K 9 7	(44)	K 9
K Q 4	4		7		K J 7 4
A J T 6 5	A J T 6 5 2		A T 6 5		A J T 6 5 2
A	A J 7 5 3		A Q 9 5		7
45	**46**		**49**		**80**
(45) (54)	(47) (58)		(44) (47)		(56) (65)
(55)	(63) (109)		(67)		(68)

1C Openings

(22)	K 9 7	A 9	(23)	K 2	K 9 2	A T 7
	K 8 7	K Q 7		K J 7	K J 4	K J 7 4
	A J 5	A T 2		J 6 5	A	–
	A Q J 3	Q J 9 7 3		A J 9 7 3	A J 9 7 5 3	A Q 9 7 5 3
	21	**26**		**31**	**35**	**36**
	(47) (52)	(44) (56)		(49) (52)	(44) (47)	(50) (54)
	(60)	(63) (70)		(66)	(67)	(60)

A	A K T 7 2	A K	(25)	A T 9 7
K 8	Q 8	7 3		K J 7 4
A J T 6	T	A T 6 2		5
A Q J 9 5 3	A J 9 5 3	A J 9 7 5		A J 5 3
37	**39**	**40**		**48**
(45) (54)	(51) (52)	(55) (59)		(53) (58)
(55) (62)	(61)	(68)		(65) (71)
(107)				

Responding Hands

(27)	(27)	(28)	(30)
Q J 6	Q J 6	Q 8 4 3	J 5
T 9 5	A T 5	A T	A T 9
K 9 7 4	K 9 7 3	Q 7 4 3	K Q 7 3
K 6 2	K T 4	K T 6	K T 8 4
52	**53**	**54**	**56**
(37) (44)	(40) (45)	(31) (38)	(41) (49)
	(107)	(46) (47)	(50)
		(48) (109)	

		(31)	
Q 8 6 3	Q 8 4	8 6 4 3	8 3
A T 9	A T 9 5	T 9 6 5	A 5
K Q 8 4	K Q 9 3	K 9 3	Q 9 8 7 4 3
K T	K 8	K 8	T 8 4
57	**58**	**59**	**60**
(41) (50)	(51) (52)	(36) (53)	(37) (54)
(51)		(52)	

(33)			(34)
Q 8 6 5 4 3	Q 6 5	Q J	–
A 5	A T 9 5 2	A 9 2	A 9
Q 7 4	K Q 7	K 9 8 7 4 3	K Q 9 8 7 4 3
K T	K 4	K T	K T 8 6
62	**63**	**64**	**65**
(39) (55)	(42) (57)	(42) (58)	(41) (59)
(56)	(56)	(108) (130)	(60)

	(37)		(40)
8 6	J 3	8 6	Q J 8 6 5 3
A T 9 6 2	A 5	A 9 6 5 2	A 2
K 9 7	K 9 8 7 4 3	K 9 7	7 3
K T 8	T 8 4	T 8 6	K T 8
67	**68**	**69**	**70**
(38) (61)	(61) (62)	(62) (63)	(63) (64)
(60)			(131)

	(41)		(42)	
Q 8	Q 8 4	Q J 6	J 6 5 4 3	Q J 8
A T 5	A T 9 5	A 9 6	A T 5	A T 9 6 5 2
9 3	K Q 7	Q 8 7 3	K 7	K Q 9
K T 8 6 4 2	8 4 2	K 8 2	K T 8	6
71	**72**	**73**	**74**	**75**
(65)	(66)	(67)	(68)	(68) (69)

		(45)	
Q J 8 5			Q 8
–			A
K Q 8			K Q 8 7 4
K T 8 6 4 2			K 8 6 4 2
76			**77**
(70)			(71)

REMAINING HANDS

(14)					
	K J 8 3	K Q J 8 3	A	T 8 4	J T 7 5 3
	Q 7 4	Q 7 4	Q T 9 7 4 3	K	A K
	T 6 5	6 5	K T 6 5	A Q 8 7 5	Q T 8 6
	J 8 4	Q J 4	K 4	J 8 6 4	A Q
	1	**2**	**3**	**4**	**5**
		(17)	(17)		(15) (17)

			(19)		
A J 7 6 4	A Q 7	7		K 5	T 8
T 9	K Q J 6	A K Q T 8 7 6 3		T 3	J 9 7
A K 7 4	K Q 8	–		A Q T 9 8 3	J T 9 7
A 3	A K Q	K Q J 6		6 5 4	K 7 3 2
6	**7**	**8**		**A**	**B**
(15)	(15) (18)	(15) (17) (18)			

Q 9 3	9 4 3	A T 7 4 2	2	J 8 6
Q 5	A K T 8 3	9	Q 7	A K J 8 7 6 4 2
K 7 5 2	6 2	J 6 4	A K 5 2	–
J 8 3 2	T 8 6	Q T 9 7	A Q T 9 8 5	A K
C	**D**	**E**	**F**	**G**

K Q 7 6 3	K Q 5 3	A J T 8 5 4	9 7 6	9	A T 4 2
A K 2	Q 8 7	9 8 4 3	J 4 3 2	J T 6 5	9 5
J 9	8	8 7	J 6 5 2	Q T 6 4 3	K Q T 9 3
K J 6	K J 7 6 5	7	9 3	4 3 2	8 4
H	**J**	**K**	**L**	**M**	**N**

A T 9 5	J 8	K 8 7	K Q 5	Q 6 4 3	A J 7 6 2
7 6 4	A K T 6	9 8	6 4 2	K Q T 5 2	Q 5
K T 8	A 7 4	A Q 9 2	A 4 3	7 6	K Q 8 5
A J 3	A Q T 2	K Q 8 7	A Q J 5	T 2	9 4
P	**Q**	**R**	**S**	**T**	**U**

J 2	(20)	A T 9	A K 9	(21)	K 7 2	(23)	K J 9 6 5 3
A J 3		K 8 7 4	K J 8 7		K Q J		8
J 5 4 3		A T 6	A J 5		J T 5		–
9 6 5 4		Q J 5	J 9 5		A J 9 3		A K Q 7 3 2
V		**9**	**10**		**13**		**27**

8	K J 9 6 5 3	–	J 8 6 5 4 3
K J 9 6 5 3	K J 7 3 2	T 8 6 5 4	9 2
A K Q 7 3 2	A	K J 9 6 5 3	9 7 4
–	8	A K	6 4
28	**29**	**30**	**61**

(73)	A K Q 8 6 3	7	(74)	A K Q 5	(75)	A K Q J 9 3
	A K T 7 6 4	9 8 5 3 2		K Q J 9		K Q J
	5	A 9 7 2		A K Q 7		A K Q
	–	8 6 3		3		A
	85	**86**		**87**		**88**

K Q J	A	A K 8 7 4	K Q 7	8	5
A J	K Q J 7	K Q J 4	A K Q 8	A K 9 7 5	K J T 2
K J 3	A Q J 6 2	A K Q J	A Q J	A Q 9	A K Q J
A K Q 7 3	A K J	–	A Q J	A K Q 5	A K Q J
89	**90**	**91**	**92**	**93**	**94**

A K Q 8 6 3	(76)	A J T 7 2	9 6 5	Q 6
A K Q 7 6 4		Q J 6	5	Q 9 8 6 4 3 2
A		8 3	9 8 4	J 5
–		7 6 5	J T 9 7 5 4	J 6
95		**96**	**97**	**98**

9	K 3	A J 8 5	K J 4	8 7
8 7 5	K 7 2	Q J 8 3	A 7 5 2	6 5
A K Q J 9 5	K 8 5 4 2	6	9 8 6 5	J 8 6 5
6 4 2	Q 7 5	Q T 7 6	Q 8	A K 8 3 2
99	**100**	**101**	**102**	**103**

(78)	A K Q J 8 7 4	(80)	A K Q 8 6 3	A	A K T 9 8
	K Q J T 9 3		A K T 7 6 4	K Q J T 9 7	K Q J T
	–		5	Q J T 8	A Q T
	–		–	A 3	5
	104		**105**	**106**	**107**

4	8 7	(81)	Q 9 6 4	K 4 2	K J T 3
A Q 8	J		J 7 5 4	9 8 6	T 5
A K J 6 5 3 2	A K Q T 9		2	5 2	Q J 6 4
K 7	A K Q J 5		K 8 6 4	A Q 9 5 3	K 8 7
108	**109**		**110**	**111**	**112**

A 9	(83)	Q T 7 6 4 2	4 3	8 7	Q 5
Q J 9 7 5		Q 8 5	K J T 7 5 4	Q T 9	K 9 5
7 6 5		7 6	K 4	J T 6 3	K 8 4 2
J 8 5		T 6	J 7 3	J 9 8 4	Q T 7 2
113		**114**	**115**	**116**	**117**

J T 6 5	A J 9 6 5	J T 6 5	A K 8 7 6	9 8
9 3	Q 9 5 4	4	5 3	A Q J 8 7 3
Q J 9 6	7 6	J 9 6 2	J T 5 3	A 6 3
J 8 4	J 8	K 5 4 2	9 5	6 3
118	**119**	**120**	**121**	**122**

8 7	(84)	9	3
6 4		K Q J 8 7 6 5 4	–
K Q J 8 7 6		T 8 7	K J 9 7 6 4 3 2
K 7 2		5	Q J T 5
123		**124**	**125**
		(87)	(87) (89)
			(97)

(85)	A Q J 4 3	A T 4	(87)	K J T 4	5 3
	K Q 7 5 2	9 7 3		Q J 9 8 5 3 2	J T 9 7 5 3 2
	Q	A Q T		–	A K
	K 3	A K 8 6		T 4	T 3
	126	**127**		**128**	**129**

(88)	K 7	7	(89)	K 8
	7 4	8 5 2		A Q J T 8 7 4 3
	A K Q T 8 4	T 7		–
	9 6 5	A K Q J 7 5 3		9 8 5
	130	**131**		**132**

(91)	A Q T 7 4	T 7 2	(92)	K Q J T 9 8	Q 8 7 6 4
	K J 6	9 5 4		4 3 2	K 7 6
	Q 8 5	Q 9 7 3		4 3	J 6 5
	6 2	J 9 5		4 2	9 8
	133	**134**		**135**	**136**
	(94)			(93)	

(96)	K Q J T 6 5	A 7	9	8 3
	A Q 9	A K T	6 5	K Q J T 9 7 6 5
	K 4 3	4 2	K Q J 9 7 6 5	9 6 3
	2	A Q T 7 6 3	A K 2	–
	137	**138**	**139**	**140**
				(97)

(97)	A Q 8	K 7 3	9 5 4	J T 6 2	(98)	A Q 6
	K J 6 5	A Q 9 7	T 8 3 2	4		7 2
	7 2	J 5 4	9 8 6 3	A K Q T		A K Q 4
	T 9 5 3	A 4 2	Q 7	K J 8 6		Q 9 6 2
	141	**142**	**143**	**144**		**145**

K J 9 3	A J 9 5	K J 6	A K T	Q T 9 7	K 6
6 5	K 6 4	K 8 6 4	K Q 9	A K J 7	Q 8
8 6 3	K T 8	A J 5	Q J 9 2	J T	A K Q T 9
A K 8 5	A J 3	A J 5	K T 3	A Q T	K 9 7 5
146	**147**	**148**	**149**	**150**	**151**

A Q J T 8	(99)	A K 9 7	K 8 7	J 9 5 3	A 8 6 4 3	Q J 8 7
K 9		7	9 8	Q	–	2
Q T 9		A T 6 5	A Q 9 2	A J 7 3 2	K 8 6 4	Q J T 3
A 8 7		A Q 9 5	K Q 8 7	A Q 6	A Q T 4	A K J 5
152		**153**	**154**	**155**	**156**	**157**
					(101)	

(100)	K T	(101)	8 6 4	K Q	Q 9 8	K J 9 8
	K Q T 8 7 6		9 8 5 3	8 2	K Q 9 2	K Q 9 2
	9 5 4		8 4 3	Q J T 5 3 2	Q J 8 2	K 6 5
	8 5		Q 8 4	9 5 2	Q 6	5 2
	158		**159**	**160**	**161**	**162**

(104)		(106)	
A Q 8	A K Q T 7 4 3	A K Q J 9 6 3	7 2
A K Q J 3	A	A K	–
K Q T 9 8	K Q	8	A K Q J T 5 4
–	K Q 6	7 5 4	9 8 6 2
163	**164**	**165**	**166**

			(110)
7 2	A 9 7	K 6 3	A K 8
9 8 6 2	K 8 5 4	A 9 2	A J T
A K Q J T 5 4	K 7 4	A 8 3 2	A 9 4
–	A 7 5	K 6 3	K J T 7
167	**168**	**169**	**170**

			(111)
K Q J	Q J 8	A K 8 7	A
A T 9	A K T	A Q J 3	K 7
A K 8 5	A Q 9 3	A K Q	K Q J T 8 5 4 2
K J T	A K J	K 4	K 3
171	**172**	**173**	**174**

(113)
A J T 7
A K Q J T 9
A K 9
–
175

Glossary

Acol A well-known and popular English system of bidding named after the club where it was developed.
Alert When a conventional, i.e. 'unnatural' bid is made by a player it should be alerted (a tap on the table) by the player's partner. An opponent wishing to know the meaning of the bid (as with any bid) may then ask, when it is the turn of that opponent to call.
Asking bid A bid which asks partner for specific information and which may be quite unrelated to the denomination used.
Auction The bidding sequence between the deal and commencement of play.

Balanced hand	4 3 3 3	A hand having no long and no short suits.
	4 4 3 2	
	5 3 3 2	
Semi-balanced	5 4 2 2	
	6 3 2 2	

Unbalanced Any other shape.
Blackwood An ace asking bid named after its inventor, Easley Blackwood.
Bid A call which contains a number and a denomination, for example 2H, 1NT.
Biddable suit One containing four or more cards.
Bidding space The available bids in an auction, from 1C to 7NT.
Call Any bid, double, redouble, or pass.
Communication The ability to cross from one hand of a partnership to the other, during the play.
Competitive bid A bid made in a competitive situation, designed either to secure the contract or to push the opponents one higher.
Constructive bid A bid, the main aim of which is to help the partnership reach a makeable contract.
Contested auction An auction where each side makes at least one bid.
Contract Is determined by the final bid in the auction and any subsequent doubles or redoubles.
Control A card or shortage in a suit which limits the opponents to no more than one trick in that suit.
Convention An agreed definition of a bid which is not its natural one. The bid becomes 'artificial'. *See* Blackwood, Stayman. Such a bid must be alerted when appropriate.

Cue bids In a competitive situation a cue bid is a bid in the opponents' suit, which is forcing. In an uncontested auction it is a bid of a new suit when trumps have been agreed to show a control in that suit.
Deal The shuffling, and sharing one by one to each player, of the fifty-two cards in the pack.
Declarer The member in the partnership winning the contract who first made a bid in the final denomination. Plays both his or her hand, and dummy's hand.
Destructive bid A bid, the primary purpose of which is to disrupt the opponents' bidding.
Director The person in charge of a bridge event.
Discard (When a player is unable to follow suit.) The card played from another suit *which is not a trump.*
Distribution The way in which the cards lie, within any hand, and within the whole deal. Elements of the distribution are the lengths of the suits, and where (say) aces lie in relation to kings.
Double A call which seeks to penalise opponents when used naturally, but is often used conventionally.
Double dummy An examination of the deal with all the cards face up.
Doubleton A holding of exactly two cards in a suit.
Dummy In strict parlance, declarer's partner, who 'sits like a dummy'. Now also used to describe the hand which that player lays face upwards on the table to be played by declarer.
Duplicate bridge Where hands are duplicated so that all the pairs in a competition play the same hands in order to gain fair comparison in measuring performance.
Duplicated values When, for example, a doubleton AQ sits opposite the doubleton KJ; the partnership holds the four top cards in the suit, but can only achieve two tricks from them.
Entry A winning card in a hand which can be used to gain entry into that hand.
Finesse A play seeking advantageous distribution of the card(s) higher than the card played, or the card played to.
Fit When both partners have sufficient holdings in the same suit to enable them to use it as a trump suit.
Forcing bid or rebid A bid, or rebid, which the partner of the bidder may not pass unless the next opponent intervenes.
Fourth in hand The fourth player at the table in calling order for that hand.
Game A made contract, or series of successful part scores, scoring 100 or more.
Gerber A bid of 4C which asks for aces. Named after its inventor.
Grand slam Thirteen tricks bid for in a single contract.

Grand slam force A bid of 5NT requiring partner to bid seven with two of the top three honours in the suit agreed, and to bid six otherwise.
Guard A holding in an opponent's suit which enables you to obtain the lead and prevent the suit being run.
Honour Any A, K, Q, J, T.
Intervention The insertion of a bid or take out double at any stage in the auction by the opponents of the opener.
Invitational bid A bid which invites partner to consider a game rather than a part score, or a slam rather than a game, if partner is at the top of the range shown so far.
Jump bid A bid which is made at a higher level than is necessary.
Jump overcall An overcall at one level higher than is necessary.
Lavinthal The name of a player which has been attached to informative discards and signals suggested by him.
Lead The first card played of the four cards constituting a trick. To be played by the winner of the previous trick unless it is the opening lead.
Length Refers to the number of cards held in a suit.
Limit bid A bid which narrows a hand to within a given point range.
Line of play The way a declarer chooses to play the contract.
Major suit Spades, Hearts. Each trick made in a successful undoubled contract scores thirty points.
Match points A popular method of comparing the results on a hand in a duplicate session.
McKenney The name of a player which has been attached to informative discards and signals suggested by him.
Mirror distribution When the hands in a partnership have duplicated suit lengths.
Minor suit Diamonds, Clubs. Each trick made in a successful undoubled contract scores twenty points.
Misfit When partners have shortages in each other's long suit(s).
Negative response A bid which, in answer to partner's forcing bid, declares the hand to be lacking by specific criteria.
Not vulnerable Being without a game in a rubber in play.
Opening lead The first card played to the first trick. The only card played without full knowledge of dummy's holding. It should be played by the player sitting on declarer's left.
Overcall An intervening bid, made after the opponents have opened the bidding.
Over ruff The play of a higher trump than one already used by another player to ruff.
Over trick Any trick made over and beyond the tricks contracted for.

Part score A score made from a successful contract which is less than 100 points, the value of game.
Partner The person, fortunate or unfortunate, who sits opposite you at the table.
Partnership Two players sitting either NS or EW.
Phantom sacrifice A sacrifice bid made when the contract the opponents had reached was unmakeable.
Playing strength The strength of a hand measured in playing tricks.
Playing trick A trick which one can expect to make in the play when playing in one's preferred denomination (normally a suit).
Positive response A bid which, in answer to partner's forcing bid, declares the hand to meet specific criteria.
Pre-emptive bid A bid which rapidly escalates the bidding, in order to deny bidding space to the opposition.
Rebid A second or further bid made by a player who has already bid.
Rebiddable suit Usually a suit containing five or more cards.
Redouble Can only follow a double, and increases penalties and bonuses even further.
Response A bid made in reply to opener's or overcaller's bid.
Reverse bid It is a rebid in a new suit after a simple response which forces partner to give preference to the original suit at the three level.
Revoke When a player plays a card to a trick which is not of the same suit as the card led, when that player does hold a card of the suit led.
Rubber Winning the best of three games.

Bonuses are:	contested rubber	(2,1)	500
	uncontested rubber	(2,0)	700.

Rubber bridge is normally played for so much a hundred.
Ruff A trump card played on a trick where one of the other three suits was led.
Rule of 2 and 3 A way of judging the safety level of a pre-emptive bid. Originally due to Culbertson.
Sacrifice A contract intended, in going down, to give opponents a lesser score than their own contract would produce.
Side suit A suit other than the trump suit.
Signals High, intermediate, or low cards of particular suits used to convey information to partner in order to further the defence.
Single suited hand A hand which contains only one biddable suit.
Singleton A holding of exactly one card in a suit.
Small slam Twelve tricks bid for in a single contract.
Solid suit A (long) suit where no losers are expected.
Stayman A conventional bid of 2C in response to partner's opening no trump bid, named after its inventor. It asks opener about major suit holdings.

Stopper *See* Guard.
System The set of agreed meanings which attach to the calls which a partnership might use during the auction.
System card A written card with the partnership system summarised neatly and completely.
Table An alternative term for dummy. One speaks of 'playing from the table'.
Take out double A conventional use of a double, asking partner to bid.
Tenace A holding of two separated honour cards in one suit, neither being of necessity an ace or a ten.
Third in hand The third player at the table in calling order for that hand.
Three-suited hand An unbalanced hand containing three biddable suits. One may be rebiddable.
Timing Contriving to play cards in the hand at the most advantageous time.
Touching suits Suits which are next to each other in rank, for example diamonds, hearts.
Two-suited hand An unbalanced hand holding two biddable suits, with at least one being rebiddable.
Under trick Any trick not made which was contracted for.
Void Having no cards at all in a suit.
Vulnerable Having made one game in the rubber in play.